Since I Left You

33 1/3 Global

33 1/3 Global, a series related to but independent from **33 1/3**, takes the format of the original series of short, music-based books and brings the focus to music throughout the world. With initial volumes focusing on Japanese and Brazilian music, the series will also include volumes on the popular music of Australia/Oceania, Europe, Africa, the Middle East, and more.

33 1/3 Japan

Series Editor: Noriko Manabe

Spanning a range of artists and genres—from the 1970s rock of Happy End to technopop band Yellow Magic Orchestra, the Shibuya-kei of Cornelius, classic anime series *Cowboy Bebop*, J-Pop/EDM hybrid Perfume, and vocaloid star Hatsune Miku—33 1/3 Japan is a series devoted to in-depth examination of Japanese popular music of the twentieth and twenty-first centuries.

Published Titles:
Supercell's *Supercell* by Keisuke Yamada
AKB48 by Patrick W. Galbraith and Jason G. Karlin
Yoko Kanno's *Cowboy Bebop Soundtrack* by Rose Bridges
Perfume's *Game* by Patrick St. Michel
Cornelius's *Fantasma* by Martin Roberts
Joe Hisaishi's *My Neighbor Totoro: Soundtrack* by Kunio Hara
Shonen Knife's *Happy Hour* by Brooke McCorkle
Nenes' *Koza Dabasa* by Henry Johnson
Yuming's *The 14th Moon* by Lasse Lehtonen
Toshiko Akiyoshi-Lew Tabackin Big Band's *Kogun* by E. Taylor Atkins

Forthcoming Titles:
Yellow Magic Orchestra's *Yellow Magic Orchestra* by Toshiyuki Ohwada
Kohaku utagassen: The Red and White Song Contest by Shelley Brunt
S.O.B.'s *Don't Be Swindle* by Mahon Murphy and Ran Zwigenberg

33 1/3 Brazil

Series Editor: Jason Stanyek

Covering the genres of samba, tropicália, rock, hip hop, forró, bossa nova, heavy metal and funk, among others, 33 1/3 Brazil is a series devoted to in-depth examination of the most important Brazilian albums of the twentieth and twenty-first centuries.

Published Titles:
Caetano Veloso's *A Foreign Sound* by Barbara Browning
Tim Maia's *Tim Maia Racional Vols. 1 & 2* by Allen Thayer
João Gilberto and Stan Getz's *Getz/Gilberto* by Brian McCann
Gilberto Gil's *Refazenda* by Marc A. Hertzman
Dona Ivone Lara's *Sorriso Negro* by Mila Burns
Milton Nascimento and Lô Borges's *The Corner Club* by Jonathon Grasse
Racionais MCs' *Sobrevivendo no Inferno* by Derek Pardue
Naná Vasconcelos's *Saudades* by Daniel B. Sharp
Chico Buarque's First *Chico Buarque* by Charles A. Perrone

Forthcoming titles:
Jorge Ben Jor's *África Brasil* by Frederick J. Moehn

33 1/3 Europe

Series Editor: Fabian Holt

Spanning a range of artists and genres, 33 1/3 Europe offers engaging accounts of popular and culturally significant albums of Continental Europe and the North Atlantic from the twentieth and twenty-first centuries.

Published Titles:
Darkthrone's *A Blaze in the Northern Sky* by Ross Hagen
Ivo Papazov's *Balkanology* by Carol Silverman
Heiner Müller and Heiner Goebbels's *Wolokolamsker Chaussee* by Philip V. Bohlman

Modeselektor's *Happy Birthday!* by Sean Nye
Mercyful Fate's *Don't Break the Oath* by Henrik Marstal
Bea Playa's *I'll Be Your Plaything* by Anna Szemere and András Rónai
Various Artists' *DJs do Guetto* by Richard Elliott
Czesław Niemen's *Niemen Enigmatic* by Ewa Mazierska and Mariusz Gradowski
Massada's *Astaganaga* by Lutgard Mutsaers
Los Rodriguez's *Sin Documentos* by Fernán del Val and Héctor Fouce
Édith Piaf's *Récital 1961* by David Looseley
Nuovo Canzoniere Italiano's *Bella Ciao* by Jacopo Tomatis
Iannis Xenakis's *Persepolis* by Aram Yardumian
Vopli Vidopliassova's *Tantsi* by Maria Sonevytsky
Amália Rodrigues's *Amália at the Olympia* by Lila Ellen Gray
Ardit Gjebrea's *Projekt Jon* by Nicholas Tochka
Aqua's *Aquarium* by C.C. McKee
Einstürzende Neubauten's *Kollaps* by Melle Jan Kromhout and Jan Nieuwenhuis
J.M.K.E.'s *To the Cold Land* by Brigitta Davidjants

Forthcoming Titles:
Taco Hemingway's *Jarmark* by Kamila Rymajdo
Tripes' *Kefali Gemato Hrisafi* by Dafni Tragaki
Silly's *Februar* by Michael Rauhut
CCCP's *Fedeli Alla Linea's 1964–1985 Affinità-Divergenze Fra Il Compagno Togliatti E Noi Del Conseguimento Della Maggiore Età* by Giacomo Bottà

33 1/3 Oceania

Series Editors: Jon Stratton (senior editor) and Jon Dale (specializing in books on albums from Aotearoa/New Zealand)

Spanning a range of artists and genres from Australian Indigenous artists to Maori and Pasifika artists, from Aotearoa/New Zealand noise music to Australian rock, and including music from Papua and other Pacific islands, 33 1/3 Oceania offers exciting accounts of albums that illustrate the wide range of music made in the Oceania region.

Published Titles:

John Farnham's *Whispering Jack* by Graeme Turner
The Church's *Starfish* by Chris Gibson
Regurgitator's *Unit* by Lachlan Goold and Lauren Istvandity
Kylie Minogue's *Kylie* by Adrian Renzo and Liz Giuffre
Alastair Riddell's *Space Waltz* by Ian Chapman
Hunters & Collectors's *Human Frailty* by Jon Stratton
The Front Lawn's *Songs from the Front Lawn* by Matthew Bannister
Bic Runga's *Drive* by Henry Johnson
The Dead C's *Clyma est mort* by Darren Jorgensen
Ed Kuepper's *Honey Steel's Gold* by John Encarnacao
Chain's *Toward the Blues* by Peter Beilharz
Hilltop Hoods' *The Calling* by Dianne Rodger
Screamfeeder's *Kitten Licks* by Ben Green and Ian Rogers
Soundtrack from *Saturday Night Fever* by Clinton Walker
The Avalanches' *Since I Left You* by Charles Fairchild
The Clean's *Boodle Boodle Boodle* by Geoff Stahl
John Sangster's *Lord of the Rings, Vols. 1-3* by Bruce Johnson

Forthcoming Titles:

The Triffids' *Born Sandy Devotional* by Christina Ballico
Crowded House's *Together Alone* by Barnaby Smith
5MMM's *Compilation Album of Adelaide Bands 1980* by Collette Snowden
INXS' *Kick* by Ryan Daniel and Lauren Moxey
Sunnyboys' *Sunnyboys* by Stephen Bruel
Eyeliner's *BUY NOW* by Michael Brown
silverchair's *Frogstomp* by Jay Daniel Thompson
TISM's *Machiavelli and the Four Seasons* by Tyler Jenke
The La De Das' *The Happy Prince* by John Tebbutt
Gary Shearston's *Dingo* by Peter Mills

33 1/3 South Asia

Series Editor: Natalie Sarrazin

From the films of Bollywood and Lollywood, to home-grown *bhangra* hip-hop, Hindu devotional pop and Sufi rock, Sri Lankan rap, Indo jazz and disco, new-wave electronica and diasporic Asian Underground scene, 33 1/3 South Asia takes readers on a sonically diverse journey through the most significant soundtracks and albums from the twentieth and twenty-first centuries.

Published:

Dil Chahta Hai Soundtrack by Jayson Beaster-Jones

Lata Mangeshkar's *My Favourites, Volume 2* by Anirudha Bhattacharjee and Chandrashekhar Rao

Forthcoming:

Coke Studio (Season 14) by Rakae Rehman Jamil and Khadija Muzaffar

Since I Left You

Charles Fairchild

Series Editors: Jon Stratton, UniSA Creative, University of South Australia, and Jon Dale, University of Melbourne, Australia

BLOOMSBURY ACADEMIC
NEW YORK • LONDON • OXFORD • NEW DELHI • SYDNEY

BLOOMSBURY ACADEMIC
Bloomsbury Publishing Inc
1385 Broadway, New York, NY 10018, USA
50 Bedford Square, London, WC1B 3DP, UK
29 Earlsfort Terrace, Dublin 2, Ireland

BLOOMSBURY, BLOOMSBURY ACADEMIC and the Diana
logo are trademarks of Bloomsbury Publishing Plc

First published in the United States of America 2025

Copyright © Charles Fairchild, 2025

All rights reserved. No part of this publication may be
reproduced or transmitted in any form or by any means,
electronic or mechanical, including photocopying, recording,
or any information storage or retrieval system, without
prior permission in writing from the publishers.

Bloomsbury Publishing Inc does not have any control over, or
responsibility for, any third-party websites referred to or in this book. All
internet addresses given in this book were correct at the time of going
to press. The author and publisher regret any inconvenience caused if
addresses have changed or sites have ceased to exist, but can accept no
responsibility for any such changes.

Whilst every effort has been made to locate copyright holders
the publishers would be grateful to hear from any person(s)
not here acknowledged.

Library of Congress Cataloging-in-Publication Data
Names: Fairchild, Charles, 1967- author.
Title: Since I left you / Charles Fairchild.
Other titles: Avalanches' Since I left you
Description: [1.] | New York : Bloomsbury Academic, 2025. | Series: 33 1/3
Oceania | Includes bibliographical references and index.
Identifiers: LCCN 2024024350 (print) | LCCN 2024024351 (ebook) | ISBN
9798765115510 (paperback) | ISBN 9798765115527 (hardback) | ISBN
9798765115534 (ebook) | ISBN 9798765115541 (pdf)
Subjects: LCSH: Avalanches (Electronica group). Since I left you. | Popular
music–Australia–History and criticism. | Electronica
(Music)–Australia–History and criticism.
Classification: LCC ML421.A929 F35 2025 (print) | LCC ML421.A929
(ebook) | DDC 781.6480994–dc23/eng/20240624
LC record available at https://lccn.loc.gov/2024024350
LC ebook record available at https://lccn.loc.gov/2024024351

ISBN:	HB:	979-8-7651-1552-7
	PB:	979-8-7651-1551-0
	ePDF:	979-8-7651-1554-1
	eBook:	979-8-7651-1553-4

Typeset by Integra Software Services Pvt. Ltd.

Series: 33 1/3 Oceania

To find out more about our authors and books visit www.bloomsbury.com
and sign up for our newsletters.

Contents

Prologue x

1 **The World (in) Fragments** 1

2 **Australian Popular Music Has Always Been a World of Boundless Possibility** 13

3 **Imagining The Avalanches, 1997–2001** 37

4 **The Imaginary Avalanches, 2001–21** 55

5 **The Aesthetics of *Since I Left You*** 77

Conclusion: The Feels in the Machine 103

Bibliography 109
Index 119

Prologue

Since I Left You has a reputation among its advocates that exceeds those of nearly all of its closest peers. This album was first released in Australia in late 2000 and then overseas the following year. Its legend has only grown in the decades since its release. This is due in large part to the effusive reception it initially received. Unusually for an entirely sample-based album, it enjoyed both chart success and formal accolades from the start in Australia, North America, the UK, and Europe. The album enjoyed particular success in Australia, winning four ARIAs, charting nationally, and being honored with two Top Ten placements in the once-dominant Triple J Hottest 100, once in the year of its release, the other in the retrospective Best Australian Albums list from 2011.

Despite the inordinate amount of attention this album has received, it has never been thoroughly examined in context. While repeatedly celebrated for its artistry, technical skill, and emotional resonance, it has never been definitively placed in the world that produced it. Further, no one has tracked its emergence in the decades after its release into the kinds of presumed permanence and "timelessness" our contemporary popular culture has collectively seen fit to retrospectively bestow on those works a certain consensus marks as "great."

This book places this album in its historical, technological, and cultural contexts. It looks closely at the social and aesthetic attributes it has been said to possess. It examines how a clear set of aesthetic aspirations guided its creators. It seeks to grasp the core musical gestures the album presented. It looks at how its makers pasted together the shattered fragments of the many sound worlds they used to create it. Finally, it looks at its *national* origins. The Avalanches are Australian and that matters. This easily overlooked fact shaped much of this album's production, distribution, and consumption in subtle and sometimes elusive ways.

There is a tremendous amount known about this album. It has been the subject of a huge number of explanatory articles and online video explainers over the course of the last decade. Despite this, it is worth an extended look. This is because most of the materials produced about it, while often useful, are mostly focused on the influences of those who made it, how the samples were chosen and manipulated, or on the remarkably adulatory reception the album continues to enjoy. There is still a great deal to explore about it.

Since I Left You was produced at a moment of particular cultural and historical complexity and change that it managed to both reflect and anticipate. While the tools and techniques that produced this album were very much of their time, there are aesthetic aspirations this album displays that have become far more central to many subsequent cultures of popular music. To take just one example, the use of loops and samples to produce songs centered on grooves rather than chord progressions has become far more prominent and influential to popular music than ever before.

Despite the initially rapturous response to the album, The Avalanches did not formally release another album for sixteen years following *Since I Left You*. Yet they still managed to enjoy a lengthy bout of success that points to the remarkable persistence of the appreciation for this album. It was once commonly thought that sample-based music was too marginal to achieve lasting mainstream appreciation. The Avalanches and their peers proved this sentiment wrong. The experience of this album—its sounds, its historical links, and its expressive contours—far exceeded what were presumed to be the aesthetic limitations of electronic music at the time it was made.

1 The World (in) Fragments

The First Two Decades of *Since I Left You*

This book ranges across the full sweep of the first twenty years or so of *Since I Left You*, from the time of its creation in 2000 to the months after the release of the twentieth-anniversary edition in 2020. Almost the entirety of the musical world that created it is gone. Nearly every single thing that helped produce it has been blasted into fragments, economically, geographically, socially, and experientially, in ways few predicted.

When we compare the world of popular music from then to now, we find that this album is in many ways part of a vanished world. It was made using tools whose capabilities were quickly surpassed. It was made using techniques that have since been altered almost out of recognition. It was made under a legal code that was subsequently consumed by commercial precedents and priorities that will now only rarely accommodate works of this kind. It moved through a distribution system that has since been definitively marginalized if not rendered an antique curiosity. It reached people in media containers that now feel like relics. On the whole, people don't make music that way anymore, they don't listen to it that way anymore, and it doesn't move through the world that way anymore.

We know what has happened since. Songs now exist in an endless sea of other songs, scattered and algorithmically reorganized in a fragile and elusive relation to our demands as measured in clicks, taps, and swipes. Artists have been ushered into a boundless space brimming with other artists, the links between them tenuous and fluid. Wherever their work is placed, wherever it is offered to the public, the work of musicians exists in infinitely balkanized universes of endless "content." We are flooded with more immediately available music than we could listen to in a lifetime. Beyond even this, think of the "consumer," that person who buys and listens and makes all that meaning and value from music. That person was once a link in a chain. The connections they formed through music, at least the more immediately tangible ones, moved from the musician to the audience in a comparatively straightforward way. Eventually, the chain circled back on itself to begin again. That person today is something else entirely. They are a node in an endless network of infinite points of potential connection, a fine mesh whose primary task is to continually re-form itself almost imperceptibly in response to every act taken within the network.

We can come at a song or an album or an artist from any point in the social constellation, whether that point is historically distant or socially close or vice versa. This means that music has been, or at least often is, detached from its own history and from its once requisite material forms. It has been made into a subsidiary of the server, the modem, and the fiber optic cable. This infrastructure is prodigious. We must make use of an infinity of the endlessly replicating digital impulses through which music is brought to us just to listen to it. Every action we take is continually archived and made endlessly accessible to the system as data. All of our actions are also contained and framed by the system, a system we do not control and cannot influence except through the scope and volume of our participation in it.

The World Fragments

This great shattering does not only concern music. Socially and culturally we have been splintered into endlessly mutating digital shards, our identities parsed and continuously reformed by the many platforms we constitute that will always contain some trace of our actions. Economically, we have been so rattled and dispersed by the radical tumult of social life that there are more people moving from one place to another than ever in all of recorded history, many just seeking some moment of survival. The lives of many have become so inured to these forces, so pervasive have they become, that we had to conjugate an old word in new ways just to explain it: precarious, precarity, precariat.

It is unavoidably obvious now, but the world was already violently fragmenting when The Avalanches started work on this album. Even before 9/11, the post-Cold War era had ground itself into a surprising geopolitical incoherence that had taken hold across multiple areas of the world. While a few famous thinkers claimed that history had exhausted itself into the singular form of perfect coherence that is transatlantic liberalism, Clifford Geertz, like a few other anthropologists of modernity, argued in the other direction. He claimed that the seeming convergence of global interests that some claimed had started to form around what was purported to be the innately superior construct of Western democracy was an illusion. The end of the Cold War would not bring integration, he predicted, but disjunction and what he called "a stream of obscure divisions and strange instabilities" (Geertz, 2000: 219). And so it did. As the engine of neoliberalism reached top speed, in the form of the financialization of everything, Jodi Dean explained that rather than "the smooth world of flows heralded in the 1990s, contemporary capitalism depends on perforation, on holes and walls, on breaks and exceptions" (Dean, 2023). The end of the Cold War put some in mind of a global reunion or convergence of sorts that simply didn't happen.

Instead, we have witnessed multiple implosions of financial markets, careening recessions, with rises and falls of value that are unprecedented until the next round. As Jack Rasmus has shown, the post-Cold War world was awash in "cheap money" that resulted "inevitably in financial instability and crashes." Neoliberalism has continuously proved that "any attempt to stabilize markets ... quickly results in real economy contraction and recession" (Rasmus, 2020:107). These shaky foundations are very nearly universal. As Frank Bongiorno tells us, Australia too has gone along with the dominant prescriptions, also learning through multiple crises that in the 1980s and 1990s "the power of liberated financial markets combined with computer technology, economic liberalism and mass consumption to create something new and powerful" (Bongiorno, 2015: 255). Instead of a grand coming together, we arrived at a grand-scale dissensus. The mirror into which we had been gazing so lovingly was fractured.

Music has typically been thought of as a harbinger of these changes, a disembodied canary in a digital coal mine. But in truth the world shattered long before music did. It's just that the illusions of a seamless, coherent, and integrated world of music persisted for decades, far longer than they should have. In some ways, music has only recently caught up.

Sample-Based Music *In Situ*

Sample-based music has long been imagined by some as a kind of musical mirror held up to the fragmentation of the world. It has been seen by many as a forerunner of this new world. I argue it is something different in this book. The Avalanches did not produce a revolutionary text. Sample-based music was not a vanguard. It was an aural kaleidoscope remixing the sonic dust of an increasingly disordered world. Its makers meticulously formed the pieces they gathered into a pleasing aural paste, one particularly adept at papering over the cracks with the endless fragments mashed together and whirled into a sturdy sonic resin. Eventually, this rich resin hardened. As we will see in this book, *Since I Left You* is a gauzy, candy-colored fantasy whose creators sought to impose order where there was none so it could then seep into the listener's skin all the more effectively. It did this very well.

In mirroring our increasingly chaotic sensory experiences, we have been told, the iconoclastic artists of what was once celebrated as a kind of new music undermined our very notions of hierarchy, tradition, and order in the process. But this only holds if you don't take any interest in what its makers actually say about their work. When you listen to how artists such as The Avalanches, Danger Mouse, DJ Shadow, Girl Talk, J Dilla, or Madlib describe their work, not much of what they say is about creating incoherent jumbles of sound that move unpredictably and incomprehensibly forward. While their work may superficially seem to lack the aural profile of the works they sample, revise, dismantle, and reconstruct, this is not the case. The singular, overarching musical gesture of all of these artists' sample-based albums is to laboriously construct what feels to the listener to be an unexpected coherence from a massive range of sounds, some familiar, some obscure, some so aggressively manipulated as to make them completely unrecognizable. The primary aesthetic goal these artists execute is to take a profusion of pieces and produce a complex, evolving whole that directs the listener to hear what they want us to hear. They do not do this through lyrics or harmonies or verses and choruses. They do it through a continuously moving, evolving mass of previously existing sounds that have already been made, heard, and digested, sometimes by great masses of people, sometimes by only a tiny handful. What matters the most to these producers is that their labor, their skill, and their insights are rendered listenable and meaningful. Theirs is an aesthetic of transparent and extensive labor all of which can be heard, although not all of it can necessarily be known. As such, the sounds they extract and manipulate become theirs through their exertion, effort, and ability. Theirs is a form of aesthetic accomplishment that is achieved first and foremost through a careful, almost forensic, form of listening. This is what links them to their audiences: the presumption that we are there to listen to this music the same way they did.

It is worth it now to spend just a brief moment placing *Since I Left You* in relation to two of its most well-known and immediate peer works in this late twentieth-century context of fragmentation and disintegration. One of the more influential albums that helped create the space into which sample-based music would enter and thrive, however briefly, was DJ Shadow's *Entroducing...* from 1996. Josh Davis, DJ Shadow's given name, produced one of his work's signature gestures on the second track on the album, "Building Steam With a Grain of Salt," that tells us what this artist thought he was doing in an intriguingly semi-direct way. Over a few sprightly piano and vocal samples carefully extracted from Jeremy Storch's 1970 song "I Feel a

New Shadow," Davis placed a sample from a record entitled "Music Makers—Percussion," which was inexplicably produced by the Standard Oil Company of California. The sample was a spoken word passage about playing the drums. As the track starts, we hear the following:

> From listening to records I just knew what to do. I mainly taught myself and, you know, I did pretty well. Except there were a few mistakes … that I made that I've just recently cleared up. And I'd like to just continue to be able to express myself. As best as I can with this instrument. And I feel like I have a lot of work to do. Still, I'm a student—of the drums. And I'm also a teacher of the drums too.

As the lengthy track draws to a close, so does this oration:

> And I would like to able to continue to let what is inside of me which is, which comes from all the music that I hear, I would like for that to come out. And it's like, it's not really me that's coming, the music's coming through me.

It's hard not to hear this sober reflection on music making as Davis's own artistic manifesto. Indeed, as Sophia Maalsen has explained, his self-understanding as a crate digger aligns exactly with the words spoken by Standard Oil's percussive interlocutor. She cites the sense of "wonder" Davis found "in the potential treasure and the agentive possibilities" within and of a collection of vinyl he found early in his career. For Maalsen, Davis "is 'excavating' and 'mining' a relatively untouched resource to find hidden beats. He believes in the power of objects. He didn't select records by accident—he was directed to the ones he "was meant to pull out' by the records themselves" (Maalsen, 2019: 1–2).

Eliot Wilder confirms this when he explains how Davis "spent a good chunk of his life scavenging through what most dismiss as ephemera: the records that reside in those musty and dark used record stores. To many of us, they are less than meaningless. But to Josh Davis, they are lost souls" (Wilder, 2005: 1). As a result, Wilder notes, the album "sounded like nothing before or since—an album of beats, beauty and chaos, a sound that cuts to the very blue flame of the heart." He continues saying, Davis "took elements of hip-hop, funk, rock, ambient, psychedelia as well as found sounds, oddball spoken word clips and cut-out bin nuggets-a literal sweep of sounds that exist on planet earth-and then wrote the ultimate lesson" (Wilder, 2005:1).

We find similar themes when looking at J Dilla's *Donuts* produced just under ten years later. J Dilla, given name James Yancey, produced the work while dying of the health complications of lupus. As such, the work inevitably took on the melancholy air of a requiem. Jordan Ferguson has described the album as follows:

> [N]one of the music on the album ever resolves itself; resolution seems to be the last thing desired. Songs careen and crash into each other, starting and stopping without warning, never giving a listener the opportunity to fully enter them; just when you're getting comfortable, as you familiarize yourself with the elements in front of you and align your perspective to the workings of Dilla's mind, he flips it on you.
>
> (Ferguson, 2014:5)

For Ferguson, the album was

> a synthesis of everything [Yancey] had done to that point, taking the electro weirdness he'd favored earlier in the

decade, combining it with the rare groove sensibilities of his 90s work, blending it with the soul revivalism found in the music of chart-topping producers like Kanye West or Just Blaze, and slicing, chopping and reworking it into a sound singularly his own.

And yet, Ferguson claims that "[d]espite sounding jarring and scattershot, *Donuts* is a deceptively unified album, a work that challenges and confronts expectations, designed to be listened to in its entirety" (Ferguson, 2014: 5).

As with Davis, Yancey also produced a coherent long-form work that guided listeners through a massive array of sounds, musical, spoken, and otherwise, and entreated them to *listen*, carefully, the same way they had done, to hear what they were trying to say through their painstakingly organized works. As with Davis, Yancey too created a "private and personal record, a conversation between an artist and his instrument, which just happens to be the history of recorded music. It's the final testament of a man coming to terms with his mortality" (Ferguson, 2014: 6). Finally, Ferguson argues, "*Donuts* continues to exist as a late work in all its irascible, confrontational glory, continuing to challenge and irritate new listeners looking for insight into mortality with its occasionally impenetrable contradictions" (Ferguson, 2014: 105).

We can take at least two things away from these two key works of sample-based music, both of which are based thoroughly on what the artists actually had to say about their work. First, both artists imagined themselves forming a coherence where none was thought to exist. This coherence depended on how each established and maintained their relationships with their work and their listeners. Second, both adhered to very traditional ideas of art and used them to guide their work. These two things are evident in the way both held fast to very traditional artistic relationships between themselves and their work, themselves and their tradition of music making, and themselves and their listeners. Each did what artists of all kinds have always done at least since the onset of modernity. Each took the inextricable whirl of experience and perception we are all faced with every day and formed these into a thematically unified, technically skilled, fundamentally coherent, unified work of art. Each artist even spoke in the familiar, well-worn language of the elusive, unseen forces that guided their hands as they worked.

My main point here is that, as we will see throughout this book, all of this is true of *Since I Left You*. The Avalanches also crafted a diligent, scrupulously structured album made entirely of revised and recontextualized sounds. No one seems to know exactly how many samples they used and no one knows where they all came from. But that is part of the point. We don't need to know. We only need to listen to what they've done and recognize it for what it is: the result of an extraordinary bout of skilled labor that is meant to say something about the world. Like most art.

The Avalanches have mostly been imagined as something of an anomaly, an outlier to a mainstream narrative of Australian popular music that was shifting definitively away from the music that had been said to have dominated it in prior decades. As I said, the world that made this album is gone; the album is a sweet, hazy memory of another time. The Avalanches didn't produce another full-length album until 2016. And yet this album has persisted. It has been extolled, celebrated, and remembered. Why? Because despite it being thought to be marginal in 2000, The Avalanches were part of a future that was a lot closer than it initially appeared. But not for the reasons we have most often been told. There are aesthetic aspirations this album displays that were far more central to many cultures of popular music than they were thought to be in the late twentieth century. The worlds of electronic pop that have dominated the last few years of Western pop music are actually part of a longer story of which The Avalanches were already a part in the late 1990s. Notably, the use of loops, beats, and samples to produce songs centered on churning grooves has become far more prominent and influential to popular music at present than ever before. But as we will see, there was always more to it than that.

When The Avalanches were working on *Since I Left You*, the world was beset with illusions of a future coherence that was said to have been upon us. Some said the new digital world would be a grand coming together. It wasn't. Some said this new music was itself a grand amalgam of the past that invented a new future. It wasn't and it didn't, not quite. Instead, works like this were trying to redeem the world through meticulous collages that sought a new coherence in the world. Artists of all kinds have long tried to remake the past and form it into coherence in order to explain the present. Sample-based music was indicative of this at one historical moment, and it remains a marker of what still feels like one last moment of coherence, a symbol of the optimism of art, an optimism that has dissipated significantly since.

2 Australian Popular Music Has Always Been a World of Boundless Possibility

Australia has never really invented a demonstrably "new" tradition of popular music. There has been nothing like the blues, jazz, or funk; no ska, dub, or rock steady; no rockabilly, honky tonk, or Western swing invented in this country. Instead, pretty much all Australian popular music derives from musical traditions created elsewhere. But this does not make it all somehow merely *derivative*—far from it. Australians have literally always produced distinctly local versions of nearly every kind of music ever practiced here. Indeed, since the time the first Europeans arrived to colonize this continent and its people, anyone who has lived in Australia or come here from overseas was all, always, part of extensive geographically dispersed international cultures of popular music making. This is what has always linked Australian music to specific places spread throughout much of the rest of the world. This is what has defined it. The things typically thought to represent Australianness in songs or by musicians, the odd reference to a specific place in the lyrics or the exhibit of a particular style of *couture* or haberdashery (mostly hats and boots), are mainly the superficial emblems of a presumed collective identity. But it is the characteristic types of relationship with the larger world that have made the popular music produced here *Australian*.

Unfortunately, in the absence of celebrating the invention of any genuinely unique forms of popular music, many commentators have instead spent decades cringing at the country's output. In fact, so many cringed so hard for so long, that the gesture itself took on the shape of a recognized piece of Australia's national identity, earning itself the infamous denotation "the cultural cringe." Australian popular music was as often than not said to be an act of inorganic imitation or simulation. However, rather than presume a land populated primarily with thin, vague approximations of music found elsewhere, I am going to focus on a different way of looking at Australian popular music, one that is common enough as well. I will treat it as music made through invention, influence, and response in direct relation to the experience of the world in this place, from this place.

My point in this chapter is to make sure that we found our understanding of *Since I Left You* on its actual origins. This will prevent us from missing many of the forces that shaped it. When we dig into the history of Australian popular music, we find distinct iterations of parlor song, jazz, and patriotic balladry. We find typically Australian folk songs, country music, and bluegrass. We find versions of rock and indie not found elsewhere. We find new uses for reggae, R&B, and funk, and, of course, we find hip hop and EDM, two styles that have also been definitively international in scope, just like all of their predecessors. All of this music has been brought here from somewhere else or brought here by someone else. When it arrived, it was picked up, picked over, disassembled, and reconstructed. This is exactly what The Avalanches did. The ways they did it and the circumstances in which they did it make them an Australian band. The forms of invention that made this album go all the way back to the beginning of Australian popular music and reach all the way to the top, the national anthem itself.

Anthems, Official and Otherwise

At present, if you compared the official Australian national anthem, "Advance Australia Fair," to the most historically grounded of the many unofficial national anthems, for example, "Waltzing Matilda," you would be hard-pressed to see or hear any immediate connection between them. The former appears stately and noble, the latter loose and easy. The formal anthem has an official setting and recording whose use is determined by highly specific protocols. The latter can be played anytime, anywhere. The former just *feels* like a national anthem. The latter can't seem to escape being rendered on a loosely strummed acoustic guitar. The former hovers above everyday life, with its universal aspirations and stoic imagery. The latter is a symbolically potent song about a sheep thief who refused to be taken alive. But both songs have remarkably similar origins. In fact, they don't just come from a similar culture of music making; they come from the exact same one.

One of the more prominent and influential cultures of Australian popular music in the first part of the twentieth century was that which has loosely been called parlor song. This seemingly simple name belies a complex and diverse repertoire. It included songs that traversed myriad themes and styles and originated from several different countries and performance traditions, such as "Ol' Man River," "Song of the Volga Boatmen," and "Along the Road to Gundagai." The reason this song culture was so complex was because the world that produced was as well. As noted by the historian Christina Lubinski, global trade in the early twentieth century had reached a level of volume and integration never seen before.

> Newly available technologies in transport and communication, such as railroads, steamships and the telegraph, facilitated international travel, communication, and commerce, while the gold standard laid the basis for cross-border capital flows. The adoption of free trade and the expansion of Western imperialism led to more exchanges between imperialist countries and their colonies, which were opened up, often forcefully, to international trade.
>
> (Lubinski, 2012:67)

Sheet music, gramophones, and phonographs traveled through the economic and social networks established and maintained by colonialism to reach the far corners of the globe with impressive immediacy, regularity, and efficiency. The gramophone companies in particular worked extremely hard and fast to open every region of the globe to their products (Lubinski, 2012). Australia was no exception, proving a fertile market for recordings from all over the world (Reese, 2019).

Like most places in the world, Australia's popular music culture was transformed by the gramophone trade. As the historian Michael Denning has shown, the economic consequences of the rise to recording saw the structure and nature of the music industry shift significantly as "concert promoters and sheet music publishers" were displaced by the gramophone companies. Further, what Denning calls a new "economy of prestige" began to form in which new forms of music and institutions started to define the cultural value of music. As he demonstrates, "vernacular musics captured on recordings" became a newly important form of "symbolic currency" around the world (Denning, 2015:68).

"Advance Australia Fair" and "Waltzing Matilda," in particular show us how this widely circulating symbolic currency was adapted to local demands and produced local inflections. "Advance Australia Fair" was first published as lyrics and sheet music in 1878 by Scottish-born Peter Dodds McCormick, then resident in Melbourne. He explained his inspiration:

> One night I attended a great concert in the Exhibition Building, when all the National Anthems of the world were to be sung by a large choir with band accompaniment. This was very nicely done, but I felt very aggravated that there was not one note for Australia. On the way home in a bus, I concocted the first verse of my song and when I got home I set it to music. I first wrote it in the Tonic Sol-fa notation, then transcribed it into the old notation, and I tried it over on an instrument next morning, and found it correct.
>
> (McCormick, 1913)

The song manages to be both bright and solemn. The words speak of a land blessed with beauty and wealth overseen by a free people hailing from "Albion." The song follows the familiar verse-refrain structure of many such songs, repeatedly enjoining the listener into its optimistic, forward-moving paean to the new century.

The song quickly became an established part of the song culture that had inspired it. It was an easy fit for a song culture of patriotic, so-called "national" songs. Further, it fits particularly well with the many nostalgic ballads that often recalled older "folk" styles and expressions that extolled virtues of many lands and their impressive peoples as well as regaling listeners with more intimate allegories of everyday life. It was a song culture that managed to look both backward and forward at the same time. It was a song culture almost purpose built for what now seems to us to be a very different kind of song, "Waltzing Matilda."

"Waltzing Matilda" was originally published as a poem in 1895 by one of Australia's best-known writers, A.B. "Banjo" Patterson. He claimed he was inspired to write its verses upon hearing a tune sung by a family friend at a small gathering on a sheep station near Winton, Queensland. The song that caught his ear was said to have been based on the Scottish song "Bonnie Wood of Craigielee," with which it shares some broad similarities. When Paterson asked for a copy of the tune some months later, the singer could only produce a broad approximation that resulted in several rounds of confusion, revision, and correction. These origins eventually occasioned multiple "original" versions each drawn from their own handwritten manuscripts for years thereafter. What became the most important and influential version made no claims to authenticity. It was written by Marie Cowan on behalf of the Billy Tea Company, for which her husband worked. Cowan's recast song was printed in 1903 on the back of which was an ad for "Australia's National Drink." This nifty bit of product placement set the song on its current historical path (National Library of Australia, 2011).

Of direct interest to us here is how these two "national songs" were recorded in the 1930s. These recordings come as close as we can get to capturing the sound of this remarkably persistent and pervasive song culture. Each had already been popularized through their sheet music iterations and had remained popular right up to the time they were recorded. Their recorded versions simply expanded their renown. The artist whose work did the most to set these versions in cultural stone was Peter Dawson, by far Australia's most prominent recording artist of the first half of the twentieth century. It is from his recordings that we can hear what are probably the defining features of this song culture. Dawson first recorded "Advance Australia Fair" in 1931. In terms of orchestration, structure, and content, it matches what is thought to be the earliest known recording of the song from 1915. It begins with brief fanfare based on the main melody produced by a small orchestra led by horns and underpinned by strings and woodwinds. Dawson delivers each verse with perfect diction and melodic clarity. The song is jaunty yet dignified as it tells listeners of this wonderful "new" land, ripe for progress as it was.

Dawson's version of "Waltzing Matilda" is much the same. Credited with making the song a hit, this version also begins with a fanfare based on the main melody and moves easily into the same verse-refrain structure. The instrumentation and orchestration are pretty much identical. Here Dawson's perfect pronunciation takes on a text seemingly unsuited to it, in which words like "billibong" and "coolibah" lose any ease they might have had. This is reflective of how the song had long been at home in a world of very formal musical and textual expression and meaning, a home it would eventually leave.

The purpose of this brief historical excursion is to show how a remarkably persistent set of circumstances has long linked Australian popular music to what is an Anglo-American and European culture of vernacular music making. This culture was settled in Australia by the 1930s. It was based on more or less the same distribution and consumption infrastructure as North America, the UK, large parts of Europe, and most of their overseas possessions. It is here where the broader meanings of this music were produced through the audio and print media cultures that defined a common system of circulation.

These links have persisted despite many significant shifts in the predominance of different styles and traditions. Between the parlor ballad and The Avalanches, we can find an intriguing set of examples that can help show us the persistence of these forms of circulation and connection.

Rock, Oz and Otherwise

An obvious port of call is rock 'n' roll and its evolution into rock in Australia. Rock 'n' roll developed in Australia in a remarkably similar way as it did in a lot of other places not called Memphis or Cleveland. This culture of music making was an artifact of the geopolitical transformations of the Anglo-American and European worlds after the Second World War. As Albin Zak has shown, "throughout the early years, rock and roll was more a process transforming the pop mainstream than a concrete musical type. It was part crossover, part appropriation, part revision, part accident, and part market dynamics. It was born of the transitional turbulence that had roiled the pop scene ever since it began throwing off the conventions of the swing era" (Zak, 2010:175). All of this was true in Australia, just in a slightly distinct way.

Australia had all of the things most places needed to make rock 'n' roll. It had lots of teenagers coming of age. It was beginning to enjoy a form of economic prosperity that would transform most people's lives irrevocably. It had a lot of musicians playing something that was actually surprisingly close to rock 'n' roll in dance halls where a lot of those young people exhibited dance steps that really weren't that far from what they would do later to the structurally and harmonically simplified blues forms that rock 'n' roll produced and with which these young adults were already familiar. Beyond this, the country had its share of both big, lumbering record companies as well as small, agile ones, both of which focused their efforts on a whole crowd of ambitious musicians, managers, promoters, and media types that had a powerful interest in tapping into what became a fervent and profitable market for the teenaged dollar. That market was populated with "youth" movies, cheap records, free TV, and free radio just like everywhere else. In short, there were more ways than ever to reach young people and reach them they did. When American touring bands hit Australia, which they did far earlier and in far greater numbers than is often presumed, there were already loads of places for them to play and plenty of people who already knew their music and would come out to dance to it (see Arrow, 2009; Stockbridge, 1992).

It was this set of circumstances that set in train nearly two decades of rock made in Australia. Like any similar stretch of time, no real template, organizing theme, or overarching purpose can be easily grafted onto all of the music made during it. Bands as distinct from one another as The Easybeats, AC/DC, Cold Chisel, and Skyhooks have all said to have been distinctly Australian to varying degrees at different times for different reasons. Claims toward a distinctly populist strain of national distinction sometimes bordering on cultural nationalism came and went and then came back again (Stratton, 2007). But what persisted were the kinds of links to the world produced in this place by this place. They were produced in mostly the same ways and through the same means as everywhere else. Australia had its dominant companies, such as Albert Productions, which at one point spent a decade producing about 20 percent of the music found on Australian charts. It had its remarkably successful songwriters and producers, such as Vanda and Young, whose successes drew a long, continuous line from Swinging London to *Strictly Ballroom* (Zuel, 2014). It had its countercultural music festivals and its national radio and television shows that were determined to produce and then capture some kind of zeitgeist, one that never really stopped at the border.

There are two particularly telling examples of the persistence of the conditions I am describing that can bring this historical overview to a head: The Saints and The Scientists. Both are telling examples because the early success enjoyed by each band happened largely outside and away from the mainstream and yet were both products of the larger sets of circumstances created by that mainstream. Both bands formed in the mid-1970s, The Saints in Brisbane and The Scientists in Perth. It is hard to overstate just how out of the way these places were back then. Their respective scenes revolved around the music of so-called "garage" bands such as The Stooges, The MC5, and others retrospectively designated as "proto punk." The Saints produced their first single, "I'm Stranded," in 1976. The Scientists produced "Frantic Romantic" in 1979. While neither band had a particularly stable run, both produced songs that slotted right into the emerging international style of variously named punk, post-punk, or indie rock. Further, both were widely influential within the scenes produced by musicians who embraced the same music they did. Beyond this, they exerted their influence, not as derivative latecomers responding to a scene fully formed elsewhere, but as part of an emergent mainstream. Both bands were already responding to the music that was reaching them in markedly similar and recognizable ways as their overseas peers. This accounts for the later citations by others as to the pioneering and influential work they produced all on their own on the other side of the world (see Stafford, 2004; Stratton, 2007).

Dance, Dance Evolution

It should not be surprising, then, that the emergence of electronic dance music in Australia was definitively marked by the same forces and circumstances, as well as the attendant debates, criticisms, and rejoinders, as those that shaped the forms of music that preceded it. For many, this music, too, was merely derivative. It didn't feel right. It didn't sound right. The places where it was taken in weren't *really* the right ones, not really (Park and Northwood, 1996). The irony here is that EDM in Australia was also part of the same kinds of international cultures of popular music making that were experienced in pretty much the same ways as all of its predecessors. Unwittingly, many EDM scenesters continually reproduced the same old debates about their music being neither loyal enough to its surroundings (Australia) nor truthful enough to its origins (not Australia). But, of course, as with all of its predecessors, dance music came to Australia, took root and grew, and did so in typical ways. Most importantly, it grew into its characteristic kinds of venues through which it eventually found its audiences.

It grew first from one of the more intriguing by-products of the spread of the gramophone in the early twentieth century, a phenomenon found in port cities around the world. People would gather in bars, community halls, and ballrooms to listen to and sometimes dance to records. This happened in Lagos, Brazzaville, New Orleans, Havana, and Singapore (Denning, 2015; Stewart, 2000). Australia's biggest port cities, Sydney and Melbourne, were right there in the thick of it from the beginning. Given the particular distances people had to travel to get here, many well-known artists simply never set foot in Australia. As such, their disembodied presence was all that Australians had. This is what in part allowed recorded music societies to persist here far longer than one might have reasonably expected. They took many forms, such as formal recitals and informal listening parties. They took place in salubrious establishments and not. They could be widely advertised or entirely surreptitious. They offered experiences of music and society that were simply not available elsewhere. As with the underground clubs in France that first started spinning discs as entertainment in the 1940s (discotheques) and the pubs in the UK that allowed a few eccentrics to hire rooms, play records, and charge admission, Sydney and Melbourne had their proto-"dance clubs" as well (Brewster and Broughton, 1999). In Sydney's infamous King's Cross, for example, renowned show girls, erotic dancers, and drag queens performed to records decades before the dance halls heaving with swing and rock 'n' roll gave way to nightclubs. The venues in which they performed were intricately connected to similar ventures both overseas and across town (Bollen, 2013: 58–61). To put it simply, these places were also part of an international culture that shaped how things were made and experienced. Further, dancing or performing to records was a plainly normal and widely practiced thing in Australia. In the specific examples of drag shows, it was fostered at least in part by the widespread mainstream tolerance, acceptance, or even enthusiasm for female impersonation (Seligman, 2023; Steele, n.d.).

It should not be a surprise, then, that the mainstream world of post-1960s Australian popular music was no stranger to glitz, glamour, and a good show. The mainstream of Australian popular music always included the main stylistic influences of EDM right at the top of its charts from the early 1970s, always sitting cheek by jowl with far more well-remembered rock and indie songs. When we look at those charts, we find an audience that continuously embraced a plethora of disco hits, fizzy pop tunes, including a fair few electro pop classics, and the inevitable goofiness of novelty songs. Often, the distinctions between these different types of songs could be extremely subtle.

Title	Artist	Year	Peak
"Popcorn"	Hot Butter	(1972)	#1
"Never Never Never"	Shirley Bassey	(1973)	#1
"Dancin' (on a Saturday Night)"	Barry Blue	(1973)	#2
"Kung Fu Fighting"	Carl Douglas	(1974)	#1
"Mamma Mia"	ABBA	(1975)	#1
"I Do, I Do, I Do, I Do, I Do"	ABBA	(1975)	#1
"Love Will Keep Us Together"	The Captain and Tennille	(1975)	#1
"When Will I See You Again"	The Three Degrees	(1975)	#2
"Never Can Say Goodbye"	Gloria Gaynor	(1975)	#3
"Fernando"	ABBA	(1976)	#1
"Dancing Queen"	ABBA	(1976)	#1
"Money, Money, Money"	ABBA	(1976)	#1
"Rock Me"	ABBA	(1976)	#1
"SOS"	ABBA	(1976)	#1
"I Hate the Music"	John Paul Young	(1976)	#2
"Dance Little Lady Dance"	Tina Charles	(1977)	#4
"You"	Marcia Hines	(1977)	#2
"I Feel Love"	Donna Summer	(1977)	#1
"Don't Leave Me This Way"	Thelma Houston	(1977)	#6
"Stayin' Alive"	The Bee Gees	(1978)	#1

Title	Artist	Year	Peak
"I Can't Stand the Rain"	Eruption	(1978)	#1
"Warm Ride"	Graham Bonnet	(1978)	#2
"Macho Man"	Village People	(1978)	#3
"Love is in the Air"	John Paul Young	(1978)	#3
"Heart of Glass"	Blondie	(1979)	#1
"Le Freak"	Chic	(1979)	#1
"Knock on Wood"	Amii Stewart	(1979)	#2
"Pop Muzik"	M	(1979)	#1
"YMCA"	Village People	(1979)	#1
"Hot Stuff"	Donna Summer	(1979)	#1
"Born to Be Alive"	Patrick Hernandez	(1979)	#1
"I Will Survive"	Gloria Gaynor	(1979)	#5
"Can't Stop the Music"	Village People	(1980)	#1
"Funkytown"	Lipps Inc.	(1980)	#1
"Upside Down"	Diana Ross	(1980)	#1
"Call Me"	Blondie	(1980)	#4
"Blame It on the Boogie"	The Jacksons	(1980)	#4
"Kids in America"	Kim Wilde	(1981)	#5
"Louise (We Get It Right)"	Jona Lewie	(1981)	#2
"Gotta Pull Myself Together"	The Nolans	(1981)	#3
"Tainted Love"	Soft Cell	(1982)	#1
"Mickey"	Toni Basil	(1982)	#1

Title	Artist	Year	Peak
"You Should Hear How She Talks About You"	Melissa Manchester	(1982)	#4
"Flashdance … What a Feeling"	Irene Cara	(1983)	#1
"Billie Jean"	Michael Jackson	(1983)	#1
"Give it Up"	KC and the Sunshine Band	(1983)	#3
"Relax"	Frankie Goes to Hollywood	(1984)	#5
"Into the Groove"	Madonna	(1985)	#1
"You Spin Me Round (Like a Record)"	Dead or Alive	(1985)	#3
"Venus"	Bananarama	(1986)	#1
"Don't Leave Me This Way"	The Communards	(1986)	#2
"Hit That Perfect Beat"	Bronski Beat	(1986)	#3
"Locomotion"	Kylie Minogue	(1987)	#1
"Funkytown"	Pseudo Echo	(1987)	#1
"Respectable"	Mel and Kim	(1987)	#1
"You Keep Me Hangin' On"	Kim Wilde	(1987)	#1
"Get Outta My Dreams, Get Into My Car"	Billy Ocean	(1988)	#1
"Never Gonna Give You Up"	Rick Astley	(1988)	#1
"I Should Be So Lucky"	Kylie Minogue	(1988)	#1
"Got to Be Certain"	Kylie Minogue	(1988)	#1

Title	Artist	Year	Peak
"Doctorin' the Tardis"	The Timelords	(1988)	#2
"Push It"	Salt-N-Pepa	(1988)	#3
"Pump Up the Volume"	MARRS	(1988)	#6
"Blue Monday 1988"	New Order	(1988)	#4

Figure 1 *Chart positions in Australia of selected stylistically relevant disco, pop, electro pop, and novelty songs (1972–88). Source: Kent Music Report (AKA Australian Music Report) and ARIA End of Year Singles Chart. (Kent, 1993)*

What we see here is something of a contradiction to the continually rehearsed claims to the unchallenged historical dominance of rock in Australia (Murphie and Scheer, 1992:177). These plainly popular songs instead point us to a particular kind of complexity, dare I call it an *Australian* complexity. It is a complexity that grew from the country's odd place in the world. For example, a remake of a song such a "Popcorn" by Hot Butter, a genuine curiosity at the time, was a number 1 hit that unwittingly matched some of the structural and sonic aspects of the house and techno that came much later.[1] Also, throughout the 1970s and 1980s, the long-celebrated threads of late soul that led step by flamboyant step to disco found a comfortable home in Australia. Another thread consisted of disco and dance music from the UK and Ireland, with artists such as Barry Blue, Tina Charles, The Nolans, Jona Lewie, and Graham Bonnet, who, while obscure today, repeatedly popped with their own versions of these international sounds. And does anything more need to be said about Australia's unusually intense love affair with ABBA?

---

[1] We should not be surprised that early versions of this track have been sampled extensively.

My point is that what is important here is that even in this highly selective list, we can still easily follow a mainstream version of the evolution of Australian dance music that grew from a context that we have to acknowledge did in fact nurture it along for decades. But it wasn't simply radio airplay and record sales that did the business. On television, generations of young Australians and their parents would flock to shows such as *Countdown*, which, despite being produced by the otherwise staid public broadcaster, the ABC, accepted no half measures when it came to color and movement. Artists were not simply allowed to play dress up; they were often chosen to perform on that basis alone.[2]

Of course, other consequential forces had been stirring elsewhere this whole time which, despite their often marginal status, were still always conversant with a less restless mainstream. Among the more influential were the big dance parties put on at Sydney's Paddington Town Hall and later the more capacious Hordern Pavilion in the 1980s and 1990s (Harley and Murphie, 2007; Luckman, 2002; Murphie and Scheer, 1992). The most prominent and popular of these were put on by the Sydney Gay and Lesbian Mardi Gras: the Sleaze Ball and the Mardi Gras Party. The former began in October 1982 and has been produced every year since. It acts as a major fundraising event for the other Mardi Gras events, which began in 1978 (Cozijn, 1983; "Mardi Gras ...," 1982). Since that time, the Mardi Gras itself went from a contested and controversial street parade and protest to a worldwide destination event broadcast on national television.

---

[2] A very strong summation of the postwar history of pop music in Australia can be found in the five-part series from 2003 called *Love Is in the Air: Stories of Australian Pop* (ABC, 2003).

These parties grew from a long and elusive history of "gay parties," drag shows, and cabarets. These events, held semi-annually in high-profile venues such as The Trocadero, or weekly in private word-of-mouth gatherings, persisted and were supported by robust social networks from at least the late 1950s. Those who participated in these networks later recalled that the dance parties of the 1980s and 1990s were not that different from those they attended in earlier decades. "I don't think events change that much. They just grow bigger and more spectacular," one participant recalled. Another said, "As well as growing more spectacular, they have become much more public ... This 'going public' mirrors the development of a gay subculture and community" (Galbraith, 1986). The public culture of both the Mardi Gras Party and the Sleaze Ball were aggressively flamboyant and joyously hedonistic. One writer described the 1985 Sleaze Ball this way:

> It was as if ancient Rome had collided with a Mayan city, with Boy George as Shiva guarding the temple gates. Cecil B de Mille would have wept as the opera scale pageant swept through thousands of enthralled revellers.
>
> (Nell and Noona, 1987)

These parties always attracted extensive media attention, which in turn has routinely produced thousands, and later, tens of thousands, of participants and onlookers every year for decades.

At the same time, an adjacent set of regular dance parties were put on by the Recreational Art Team (RAT), often attracting many of the same revelers. These events had the freedom to be held further afield at more prominent places such as the Bondi Pavilion, Luna Park, and theaters such as the Balmain

Bijou. These events featured adventurous offerings, including drag shows, kabuki theatre, flamenco troupes, puppetry, mime performances, and the occasional BMX bike team, all set around a continuous dance party. The founder, Jac Vidgen, explained that his goal was to

> bring the gay and straight communities together. Call it building bridges. This way we can all party together in an interesting environment where no-one is oppressed or intimidated.
>
> (Galbraith, 1986)

These events and the ideas and social networks that shaped them were by no means confined to Sydney. Both Melbourne and Adelaide had well-known circuits and events of this kind in the 1980s as well (Galbraith, 1986). Giovanni Polizzi, one of Melbourne's most respected DJs who has performed under the stage name Papa Smurf on and off for decades, explained his experience of this world as a teenager:

Brunswick Street was pretty much the cultural street of Melbourne's rave scene … A lot of LGBT community, a lot of gays, a lot of straights, a lot of … everything. First time I ever went was the Brunswick Street Festa. [*sic*] We were 12, 13, and as you're walking down the streets, everyone's tripping, like everyone's off chops, having fun, rocking, like blue hair, green hair. There was this lady walking around with … like a whole basket of weed, and everyone's just grabbing a bar and rolling and there's people on the streets, on balcony's, DJ's, full on … And I was just like, what the hell is this? I was very scared because I had no idea what the hell it was.

(Holliday, 2021)

Polizzi describes his "first party experience" in 1995 when he was seventeen:

> You got a little kid from the Northern suburbs, right, rocking up to a gay festival, gay party. I was like a kid in a toy store. I was going crazy. I was jumping from this person to that person to there. I was hugging guys with their ass cheeks hanging out. And everyone's like, Giovans, calm down. I was like, no man, this is crazy … And they saw me like: "he's young. He's got no idea what's going on. He's having a good time" you know, in a good space or whatever. And everyone treated me like gold. And I was just like, I want to be here all the time.
>
> (Holliday, 2021)

For Pollizzi, the "gay parties for me were the best parties":

> They had artistic flair, they had culture. They were proud in who they were. They showed the world. They showed everyone: This is us, this is the way we party. You like it and you're all welcome to come. But this is who we are. And I loved it … The music was the best … Those parties are what shaped me and what shaped three-quarters of Melbourne's dance music scene today. And everyone that I know came from those parties … For me, that was like, the gates opened up.
>
> (Holliday, 2021)

By the late 1980s, big dance parties were regular events, happening for all intents and purposes simultaneously and in conjunction with similar developments in the US and the UK. As with the nightclub owners in the 1950s and 1960s, the raves and dance parties of the 1980s and 1990s happened through extensive and continuous networks of an international culture of music making long present in Australia. One hazy-eyed retrospective described the shift from the 1980s to the 1990s this way:

> The massive Hordern Pavilion and RAT parties, the thriving LGBT underground and, of course, the famous laid-back lifestyle all combined to make Sydney a prime party destination for hedonistic travellers in the late '80s. When a wave of UK expats brought a new dance groove—and new recreational drugs—into this lively landscape, it triggered a musical and cultural explosion, harnessing this energy into a rave scene that was uniquely creative, spirited and rich despite its small size and relative isolation.
>
> (Poe, 2017)

The scenes in Sydney and Melbourne wound their respective paths through secret phone numbers, private text messages, and hidden electronic bulletin boards producing a scene whose reach and power have only been equaled since by its relentless mythologization. The Australian rave scene, and the aptly named "bush doofs," became not just regular but very nearly constant features of urban life.

Inevitably, events such as the mythical Earthcore began to attract, well, everybody. One observer described how it was at the break of dawn "when the pounding psychedelic beats of the party reach a crescendo and the rave really begins; the moment the party-goers, many of them long-time Earthcore devotees, wait patiently for throughout the night." However, the story continues, the assembled,

> contrary to popular belief, are not merely your stereotypical conglomerate of ferals, hippies, or candy-ravers. Earthcore, as its organisers boast, comprises a much wider demographic, people from all social inclinations. Increasingly, the event is becoming home to many a professional; the "suit"

contingent, if you like. Doctors, lawyers, middle managers (even—dare we say—journalists) are part of the lesser-known outdoor rave enthusiasts, drawn to events such as Earthcore by a common desire to dance under the stars, be at one with nature, and perhaps above all, get away from the stresses of the urban jungle.

(Tomazin, 2000)

Events like this, which had been running for more than a decade under the informal catch-all moniker "doofs," were described in their originating form as a utopian incarnation: "an enclave of affect and meaning, a youth cultural site of voiced dissent and epiphanous experience, [a] post-rave technotribal gathering" (St. John, 2001:13). But as they grew, spread, and expanded, the fanatical idealism that lifted them off the ground with repeated bursts of color, passion, and a mooted tolerance and togetherness gave way to a bitterness that followed their "domestication," "regulation," and "commercialisation" (St. John, 2001:19). A sharp sliver of condescension was always held in reserve for the "dilettante renegades queued at the turn-styles and weekend ferals occupied the dance floor" as the "real" devotees were forced to continually seek out an "alternative to the encroaching forces of state, capital and cliché" (Harley and Murphie, 2007; see also Fenwick, 2022; Park and Northwood, 1996).

When the first national music award, an ARIA, for dance music was given to the legendary Itch-E and Scratch-E in 1995, the post-disco category of EDM was clarified and rendered official. It was formally inducted into the mainstream of Australian popular music, a place it had already tenuously held for some time. The proliferation of events, venues, artists, and audiences in the 1990s did not represent so much a sudden emergence of the new or a break with the past but more of a solidification of a world of music that had been present to varying degrees for decades.

This is the world that produced The Avalanches, one part indie rock, one part dance party. To a significant extent, *Since I Left You* was unleashed upon a world that was already more than ready to receive it.

3 Imagining The Avalanches, 1997–2001

The story of *Since I Left You* has been told over and over again, often in extraordinary detail.[1] The story has remained almost perfectly coherent from its first iterations. Rather than simply rehashing what is so easily found elsewhere, I will recount this story with an eye toward a broader understanding of this album and the circumstances that produced it. I am doing this because there is one mildly pernicious theme produced in the long afterlife of this album that just won't go away. Because the album is made of samples, it has been said by many to be "timeless in feel because it essentially exists in a vacuum, like some exotic transmission from another far more beguiling dimension" (Bell, 2021). This is, of course, just a pleasant fantasy that has been etched onto the surface of what remains for many a deeply enchanting and ambiguous recording. And, of course, the opposite is true. *Since I Left You* cannot help but be indelibly marked with the circumstances of its production. This may seem like the palest of truisms, but it's not. Between this chapter and the next, we will see two important entities come into view based on it. Both will help us understand this album. The first is the world that made this album, examined in this chapter, and the second are the endless drifts of fantasy that have piled up onto it since its release. These are examined in the

---

[1] The most detailed and lengthy recounting is a three-part podcast on Spotify (Bell, 2021).

next. When we look closely at these things, we find an album poised at the fulcrum of complex forms of both continuity and change that have remained far larger than it ever was.

What Were The Avalanches?

The first step we take is defining The Avalanches as a band, as this proves harder to do than it might seem. The Avalanches that made this album were never quite the same Avalanches that preceded or succeeded it. The band evolved continuously from its earliest days until it settled on the version that finally produced its second album, *Wildflower*, in 2016. But each step matters to us, if sometimes only in retrospect.

While the various members of what would become The Avalanches had tried their hand at a few iterations of various bands, the first recognizable group that produced the music that would get them noticed was The Pan Amateurs. Robbie Chater remembers that "we would just visit junk stores and find these cheap old guitars, we had no money, or old keyboards and we were just using whatever we could get our hands on really to make kind of noise music basically" (Bell, 2021). When I spoke to him in late 2023, Chater told me:

> For us Melbourne was a live music town and it was incredible for that. I mean there was The Tote Hotel, The Punters Club, The Esplanade, The Evelyn, and The Empress of India Hotel. And we sort of lived in a little grid where we could just walk from our little share house to all of those places and so it was rock, and sort of what was called alternative music in those days, and it was a thriving scene. So we always just dreamt of playing in those venues.

Chater described to me poring over the Melbourne street press every week seeking out as many shows and events as he could.

As The Pan Amateurs, Chater told me, he and Darren Seltmann, Gordon McQuilten, and slightly later Tony Di Blasi would spend an enormous amount of time going to see bands and then coming home and rehearsing. They produced what is now an elusive demo tape (literally, a cassette) of thirty songs, several of which would appear almost a year later on the first EP produced under the name The Avalanches. It was called *El Producto*. The transition from one to the other is key.

Chater told me that The Pan Amateurs developed as a guitar band "in parallel to [the sampling]. We were discovering samplers and stuff and we decided we were going to take this sort of music into these live rock venues, which nobody was thinking of doing at that time." He also said that in Melbourne the "live music scene was very supportive and you could get access to a stage on a Tuesday night to play, invite your friends down. Then we were sort of listening to all this other music and sort of trying to figure out a way to take that into these venues. So it was more of a supportive community around live music at that time, more so than the club venues." An important marker of this was the inclusion of Dexta (AKA DJ Dexter, Dexter Fabay) in the band. At the time, Dexta was arguably the most high-profile scratching DJ in Australia. He had represented Australia four years in a row at the DMC World DJ Championships, barely losing out one year to three-time winner DJ Craze. In performance, the ensemble would consist of drums, bass, keyboards, and turntables, with at least one of the keyboards rigged to play samples from their already finished recordings. The early hype for the band centered on what was, for the time, a unique inflection of broader, more recognizable forms of music.

All of this chimes with the recollections of Linda Bosidis, of Australia's Mushroom Records, who told journalist Steve Bell that "it was a very heady, rebellious, experimental time. You know there was anger and destruction and pushing boundaries and no structure. At the same time it was thought provoking and artistic and innovative and interesting." She had heard of The Pan Amateurs/Avalanches[2] through two friends who ran the record label that would release *El Producto*. She describes the band's live show in vivid terms:

> I mean it was unpredictable. I remember some of those early pub shows as well and even then they were developing and evolving. I remember on stage they would swap and rotate instruments and their live show was kind of party vibes. It was super loose and animated and a bit punk but it was crazy. I just remember how much fun it was and you wanted to be up front to witness it all. It was "What the hell's going on here?". I loved it. It was a time of indie alternative rock and that was massive. So there were elements of that in there. I mean people were listening to My Bloody Valentine, you know, Portishead and DJ Shadow, Stereolab and Chemical Brothers, and I guess that initially you know there was that bit of the Beastie Boys element in there.
>
> (Bell, 2021)

The move from this to the smooth resonances of *Since I Left You* came through Chater and Seltmann's increasing preoccupation with sampling. Chater had started a film

---

[2] I should note that at least three other names have been attributed to the band before they settled on The Avalanches.

course at RMIT and discovered he had access to a professional recording studio more or less whenever he wanted. The first demos were made there, and he remembers "there was an old Ensonics sampler in there that I taught myself how to use so I began sampling some of these old junk store records" (Bell, 2021). He also noted that music from groups such as The Pharcyde, De La Soul, and Dr Octagon had also started to shape their work as well. The fact that sampling was becoming a legitimately mainstream way to make music allowed them to start "making that shift from this sort of noise music to this sample based music, but in a way it feels like the same project to me" (Bell, 2021).

Importantly, Chater described to me living in a city with a welcoming range of venues and events:

> There was lots of stuff going on and I kind of feel like there was just a very do-it-yourself sort of thing. There were just parties and warehouse parties all over the place. But club music was beginning to be played and every weekend you could go, it might just be a warehouse somewhere, and listen to this music that for me was just like, I just never encountered it before, you know the energy of that kind of music. And Melbourne was such a super supportive live rock music city. That was why we just sort of followed that path naturally with this.

In the months before they began work on their first full album, Chater told me they were moving in a new direction:

> It was a weird situation where like really by the time we got to *Since I Left You*, we'd refined the sampling thing to such a point where there were no live elements remaining and it ended up primarily just being me in my bedroom making

> this other sample based universe, but there was still a group of four or five of us taking it out and playing it and it sounded completely different live by that point.

As Chater suggests, the difference between their live shows and the work being done on the new album was significant and marked a persistent tension in the band's public face for nearly the entire period preceding *Since I Left You* and for several years afterward. Songs from *El Producto*, especially those mined from their demos, such as "Rock City" and "Run DNA," were able to leave the confines of The Pan Amateurs' demo tape style and gain a wider foothold on The Avalanches' early EPs.

The evolution of their music from *El Producto* to *Since I Left You* is striking. The former reflects a distinct amalgam of rock and rap that somehow managed to defy the withering moniker "Rock-Rap." It was a kind of music leavened with a robust channel of the comparatively austere use of only a few samples at a time, usually as structural ballast for the trio of rhythmically yelled vocals that warbled, chanted, and falsettoed their way through a crisp thicket of sound. These songs exhibit the tenacious tensions of the work of artists such as The Beastie Boys and Australia's own DefWishCast. The vocals even offer a circuitous path back to late 1980s skate punk, at least of the non-thrash variety. The songs are free of any strong harmonic motion, instead creating a perpetual, ringing beat, scratched improvisations, and looped sample lines acting as bass, hook, and melody simultaneously.

The Avalanches' performances of "Run DNA" and "Rock City" on the ABC's Saturday morning music show *Recovery*, still making the rounds on YouTube, capture this ethos perfectly.[3]

---

[3] I found this performance on the YouTube channel "Mutant Renegade," but it has proliferated in various forms. https://www.youtube.com/watch?v=qwUpbpCGpcY.

This version of the band consisted of Seltmann on bass and vocals, Di Blasi on keyboards and vocals, Chater on drums (yes, actual drums), McQuilten on a sample-triggering keyboard and vocals, and Dexta providing his scratching mastery on turntables. The stage was strewn with old vinyl records that Seltmann, McQuilten, and Di Blasi would occasionally pick up and toss at each other or repeatedly hurl at the ground. The trio were engagingly energetic, each offering continuous calisthenic routines that belied the early hour.

Despite the manifest and thoroughgoing differences between *El Producto* and *Since I Left You*, the track "Rock City" hints at the near future, but only around the edges. The song begins with an easy groove of an acoustic guitar sample flowing back and forth between two major chords, overlaid with a delicate flute line, both of which are characteristic of the samples of sunshine-suffused West Coast American pop the band would sample in bulk over the ensuing months. Similarly, the last thirty seconds of the track ease us away from preceding clatter and yelling with a rhythmically clear mouth harp sample, harmonized with the low humming of what sounds like an early 1960s vocal group. These aural hints would later grow into a tide.

As we will see in the next two chapters, *Since I Left You* is defined by its very nearly universally recognized euphoric "spirit." This has been attributed to Chater's long struggle with the health complications of alcohol abuse. In the year before the album was completed, Chater's near constant drinking of spirits had taken a significant toll on his body. He told Steve Bell what happened when he decided to stop:

> I had a withdrawal seizure … and ended up in intensive care for a long time. And they thought I kind of, I wouldn't make it. And when I came out of that period and got well

again, *Since I Left You* just came pouring out. That's probably … a huge fork in the road and a dividing line between the earlier chaotic part of our musical output and then this pure expression of just sort of love and joy. I was just so happy to be free of this nightmare that I'd been stuck in for years. And just so happy to be alive. And every part of being alive felt so precious and beautiful. And this record just, just, that's why it sounds like that's what I hear when I listen to it again today.

(Bell, 2021)

Di Blasi recalls that in order to help Chater deal with the misery of his rehabilitation, he would bring samples for Chater to work on. And on Sundays he'd visit and the two would listen to what Chater had been doing. As Di Blasi remembers, "He was literally starting that record in, you know, rehab. It's awesome that you turn such a horrible experience into this euphoric, beautiful bit of art. Yeah, it's incredible … I feel like it's like just such a perfect turnaround of, you know, don't worry, things can look dark now, but look at what can happen" (Bell, 2021).

"Steve Pav" and "The Detective"

It was right at the point when work began on the album in earnest that their original demo as The Pan Amateurs caught the attention of promoter Steve Pavlovic. This would turn out to be one of the most important associations the band would ever have. "Steve Pav," as he was known, had established himself as a major concert promoter in Australia by the early 1990s. He seemed especially capable of marshalling the resources demanded by the logistical complexities of national tours by international artists in Australia and then wrangling the media attention required to make them profitable. We can see how this worked with The Avalanches through the short documentary feature produced by Film Australia called *Artzone*. The first person we see is Pavlovic himself, who explains, "One day I got this tape that came in a shitty envelope and it was all crappy and cruddy looking. I'm like wow this looks interesting. Let's put this on and I put it on it was the first thing I've heard in a long time that I was like 'Wow this is really fresh.'" He was talking about The Pan Amateurs' demo. Over the course of the fourteen-minute film we follow Seltmann, Chater, McQuilten, and Dexta, as they go out on a vinyl collecting run to Op Shops throughout the suburbs of Melbourne. In addition to fairly in-depth explanations and demonstrations of how they worked, which we will come back to in Chapter 5, we also see the band's relationship with Pavlovic develop. Pavlovic explains that rather than the standard resources to make the album, The Avalanches asked for something different:

> When they decided they wanted to make an album and we completed a deal with them, I said "Well okay we'll make a budget available to you to go record a record" and they're like "Look that's really great but what we really think we need to make the record we want to make is to be able to purchase the equipment that we can then sit in our house and work whatever hours we want," rather than going okay you've got like two weeks of studio time and in that timeframe you have to create and make your record.
>
> (Artzone, 1999)

Pavlovic was not only able to shepherd the band through the process of making and releasing the album on Pavlovic's new label Modular but make sure it grabbed other people's attention the way it had grabbed his.

The 1990s were a time for some of the more significant shifts in the music industry's estimations of what music counted as attractive to big record labels and the mass audiences they were chasing. In Australia, Pavlovic was very nearly unparalleled in his ability to grasp the potential appeal of a new band or artist, both in Australia and overseas, that might have once been considered commercially marginal, and exploit that appeal. His multiple successes up to the point he met The Avalanches clearly gave him the necessary leverage to put them into support slots for some of the biggest international artists to tour Australia at the time. It is important to note that the term "support act" or "opening band" doesn't carry the same dubious connotations in Australia that it does elsewhere, especially in places like the United States. For a band like The Avalanches, the opportunity to support The Jon Spencer Blues Explosion or Public Enemy on their Australian tours was career-making.

Chater explained to me that Pavlovic's ability to get them these gigs permanently changed the trajectory of the band. The festivals and tours he got artists into and his ability to bring a full slate of international and local artists together for combined events made a huge difference:

> It was huge for us to go to that first Big Day Out where Nirvana played; it was just incredible and especially the early Summer Sonic tours, you know, there was like Sonic Youth and Beck and The Beastie Boys and Pavement and The Breeders. That was sort of really pivotal for us ... But he helped us get early support gigs that were just a step up out of that pub scene. So we've got the support gigs for things like Beck and Public Enemy and The John Spencer Blues Explosion. We were sort of thrown in the deep end in

that regard and it was literally straight from our bedroom or our kitchen actually in the share house where Tony, Darren and I lived with the samplers and the little drum kit, and we just put this stuff and this broken gear in the back to car and drove it to the venue and all of a sudden we're playing in front of like 3000 people.

Chater described to me that this time was marked by a certain naivety and enchantment with the world the band was entering. He told me how a member of the Bomb Squad, Public Enemy's backing band, had found out when they did their soundcheck every day and "because we had this beaten up old drum kit along with our samples, he started coming down and jamming with this and playing the drums with it. I've still got some video of that actually; it was just like 'Is this really happening?'"

As the band started gaining renown, the album was also finally coming together, both musically and commercially. Another important relationship that developed as part of the process of completing the album was the band's collaboration with engineer Tony Espie. Espie mattered a great deal to the band artistically. He told Steve Bell that he was asked by the band's manager at the time to talk with them about how to complete the album. He remembers getting a cassette of the song "Since I Left You," and when he put it on in his car, he said he "just had to find somewhere to pull over. I couldn't drive. I was just like this music has never been heard before. This is something so fresh" (Bell, 2021). Espie had been an engineer and producer for dance music artists for years and found the contrast between The Avalanches and the music he ordinarily worked on enticing. For Espie, "the dance music was kind of so structured and formulaic compared to what they were doing, which was completely unpredictable." Espie says that they approached him because they "knew that I've done like hundreds of dance records during that time and they wanted someone to come to the project with that kind of background as opposed to rock." As we will see later, they picked the right person. Espie clearly loved the album:

> when you listen to it now, it sounds, it sounds beautiful, but it sounds really wild, you know, still sounds like quite adventurous, which is great after all these years that it can still have that effect.
>
> (Bell, 2021)

Commercially, the band benefited enormously from the international swell in the market for dance music and electronic pop in the UK and Australia (Eliezer, 2001). The rapid expansion of the commercial fortunes of this music, especially in the UK, meant that there was a ready-made infrastructure of publicity to drop the album into. Pavlovic used his extensive international connections to begin to grease the capitalist pumps that were now primed to move what for many was a new kind of music through their capacious attention-getting channels. Modular forged a deal with Sire Records and this began to produce results. Sire hired famed music promoters and marketers Giant Step, whose roots were in the 1990s New York hip-hop club scene. They also hired Cornerstone Promotion, the founders of which had also created *The Fader* magazine. Full DJ sets based on the album's tracks began to appear on influential radio shows such as *Morning Becomes Eclectic* in Los Angeles. Demos, bootlegs, and test pressing of several tracks were distributed to club and radio DJs in the US, the UK, and Australia. These quickly made their way into club DJ sets internationally. One test pressing was given to NME which reviewed it favorably, and went from there to the BBC's

Radio 1, as other bootlegs started oozing surreptitiously into London's dance clubs (Donovan, 2001c).

Sire also contracted the firm New Media Strategies to "inundate message boards and chat rooms with information about the band," directing clickers to several websites, still a novelty for many, to listen to demos and exclusive mixes (Hall, 2001; Paoletta, 2001). Influential English music critic Simon Reynolds remembers that

> we didn't know really anything about them. I think it just seemed to come fully formed. I mean, they had been around and been in other groups, I think, and they've done things, but you know, the records seem to just come out of nowhere. And I just know everyone on the internet seems to be talking about it on message boards and, you know, and there was a big buzz amongst music journalists about it.
>
> (Bell, 2021)

The band also benefited from marketing and promotions efforts directed by the Shortlist Music Project, sponsored by Microsoft, Tower Records, Adidas, Guitar Center Stores, hipster clothing shop Urban Outfitters, and something called the Coalition of Independent Record Stores (Olson, 2002). A great deal of this informal, aspirational distribution was a product of the decade-long expansion of the so-called "alternative" music market.

Espie was a respected and well-connected engineer in Melbourne, and his view from the console while working on finishing the album with the band offered him a unique perspective. Espie thought it was Pavlovic's faith in the band and the album that made the difference.

> For Pav at the time to turn people on with it because, you know, he was going to like A&R meetings and stuff like that

with this crazy music that didn't go like, well, how are we going to sell this? You know, that he had the faith … there was a lot to be said for his kind of support.

(Bell, 2021)

As the music began taking hold among the international cognoscenti of dance and electronic pop, a problem appeared that no one involved with the project had thought through at that point: clearing the samples. Given that the band quite reasonably imagined that this album would probably not gain the foothold on the attention of so many before it was even done, the issue of trying to clear the unknown number of samples they used could comfortably rest on the back burner. However, the "excitement in London since a limited-edition party tape compilation and a bootleg" started circulating was getting out of control, potentially attracting the untoward attention of music industry lawyers. The band's UK management was tasked with trying (and failing) to contain the excitement. Figures such as Mercury Prize–winning Badly Drawn Boy only fanned the flames, praising the band and playing their tracks at his shows (Donovan and Carew, 2000:12).

This is where their relatively newfound industry connections came in handy. Mario Caldato Jr., a fan of the band who just happened to have produced *Paul's Boutique* by The Beastie Boys, was able to put them in touch with Pat Shannahan, nicknamed "The Detective," to begin the delicate and potentially lengthy process of clearing as many recognizable samples as possible. Chater explained just a few of the problems to Bell:

> [W]e had a few problems because back then, you know, the samplers we used were so rudimentary. The samples were all saved on floppy disks. So if we didn't label a disk correctly, which often we didn't, we couldn't find the samples

> sometimes. It would just be on one of thousands of junk store records and we could never find it again.
>
> (Bell, 2021)

Shannahan was dramatically described by one journalist as "the shadowy figure working behind the scenes on some of the most innovative and legendary albums" (Coleman, 2016). Shannahan's career included work on albums by The Beastie Boys, Beck, Public Enemy, Ghostface Killah, the Chemical Brothers, Ice-T, and the Red Hot Chili Peppers. One writer explained that her sleuthing and negotiating skills "left an imperceptible imprint on 20 years of recorded music as a result, serving as the secret weapon for artists whose output can be at least partially defined by their creative sampling and taste for bottom-of-the-crate curios" (Gonsher, 2016).

Shannahan got into what was then the strange business of sample clearance through a life spent in a series of roles in the music industry, from dancer to administrative assistant to all-purpose fixer. She and her husband, also a well-connected jack of all trades, ran their business by word of mouth for decades (Coleman, 2016). She explained on several occasions how the process worked. The artist was expected to send her a track that was as close to finished as possible so the copyright owners, mostly music publishers and record labels, could hear music that was "as close to what it's going to sound like in the end as possible" (Gonsher, 2016). Then she negotiates a price, sets out the terms of use in a contract, and gets the respective parties to sign off. While she would always push for a fixed rate, as the use of samples and complete recordings become increasingly common, and lucrative, this was often not possible:

> In an ideal world, I'm looking for a flat-fee buyout, so we never have to renegotiate. But that's never gonna happen

> with a major or anyone who is sophisticated within the industry. A major will absolutely not agree to a buyout if it's just one second. They absolutely want to participate with everything down the line. So you have to deal with that. You try to get them to be as reasonable as possible, and—let me tell you—sampling is where they are the most unreasonable.
>
> (Coleman, 2016)

She did not speak particularly well of those she had been negotiating with for so long:

> Sampling comes in like a miracle. And artists' careers are suddenly being rejuvenated. James Brown, Bootsy, all these people who didn't have careers anymore. People now needed money in their older years have income coming in. This was fabulous. And the labels and have publishers have done whatever they can to kill the business. They've killed the sampling license part of the business in the last few years.
>
> (Coleman, 2016)

By contrast, Shannahan repeatedly and fulsomely praised The Avalanches. She told one writer that "The Avalanches have done what no one else has ever done." She felt that a lot of the artists she worked with "are just taking one little bit and looping it over and over. There's not a lot of creativity there." "But I LOVE the Avalanches," she said, "because I'm a melody person, and I love what they do with melodies" (Coleman, 2016).

Shannahan had a unique perch to observe the goings on around sampling in the mid- to late 1990s. She recalled that she "looked at it as a new, creative source of revenue. A source of revenue, but also a new, creative art form. There are a lot of people who have a real problem with it—they always have and they still do. They get very grumpy about sampling" (Gonsher,

2016). As part of her negotiations she tried to "explain to people for years that this is a very interesting art form, and as long as people are licensing the rights, it's a very, very interesting thing … But some people are open to it, and other people are not." For her, The Avalanches were an important test case:

> But if I can get someone on the phone who I would be dealing with, I would basically explain who the artist is—"These are the Avalanches"—and try to make them understand what creative geniuses they are, and how creatively they use the sample, too. That it's something to be really proud to be a part of, and see if I can get them to negotiate something that's reasonable.
>
> (Gonsher, 2016)

In the end, all of Pavlovic's connections, deal-making, and promotional work, as well as Shanahan's "detective" work and advocacy, paid off comparatively quickly and handsomely. Between its various staggered releases in the UK, Australia, the US, and Europe, the album and its attendant singles charted well and persisted for months across multiple charts in multiple countries. The band also enjoyed a raft of awards at the ARIAs (Australia's national music awards), the Dance Music Awards (then a separate event), and won the Video of the Year at the MTV Europe Music Awards for "Since I Left You" in 2001.

What seems to stand out from the many iterations of the story of *Since I Left You* I have read is the often intense loyalty exhibited by so many of the key people who worked in some way to make it possible and, similarly, those who felt compelled to bring it to as many parts of their worlds of music making as they could. Steve Pavlovic's mastery of the sinews and ligaments of the international music market and Pat Shannahan's extraordinary skills at putting a case to people to be reasonable are notable. Tony Espie's oft-expressed love of this music saw both him and the band through the lengthy and technically challenging process of smoothing over literally thousands of mismatched scraps of source material. Similarly, those who felt compelled to bring this music in whatever form they had to as many parts of the worlds of music making they were a part of as they could also played a crucial role in preparing the ground for its eventual ecstatic reception. The often fervent, animated endorsements from writers, critics, radio DJs, club DJs, and other musicians created a way of hearing this music that helped make it widely popular.

The world that made this album is long gone. The tools that made it are wholly obsolete, and many of them were even before the album went public. The continual expression of support for this "fresh," "new" music is clearly only of historical interest now, surpassed as it has been by so much similar music made by generations of new "fresh," young talent. The idea that this music might not have been worth the sheer investment by its principles, in terms of the significant financial risk, especially by those at the big record labels and dominant media producers, isn't a question now. While some imagined this music to have been edgy or subversive, such ideas are obsolete as well. In short, every necessary skill and resource, technical, legal, administrative, communicative, artistic, and otherwise, was brought to bear to make this thing *work*. In the next chapter, we'll dig into the content of its often rapturous reception to see exactly what this means.

4 The Imaginary Avalanches, 2001–21

In the two decades after its release, *Since I Left You* has been on a strange journey. The reception of the album began before it formally existed. The initial reactions took the form of a few anomalous reviews and reported sightings of imports, bootlegs, singles, and one-off mixes. Then, there followed a burst of intense adulation from the UK, expertly seeded by the band's various labels and promoters, when various versions of what was to become the full album reached London. That lasted a little over a year. The antics of the British music press inspired a bemused reaction in Australia (nothing new there). Throughout, there was another intermittent, mostly subterranean response emanating from the United States. It came from those who viewed themselves as the emergent deans of music writing at publications vying to become the new denominators of what counted as "important" music. All three forms of writing trundled along mostly familiar paths from the beginning of 2000 to about the end of 2002. A few stragglers brought this initial bout of engagement to a quiet end in about 2005.

But then something strange happened: nothing. The Avalanches didn't release another album for sixteen years. Unsurprisingly, the tide of interest in them went out again. However, something even stranger happened after that. After years of occasional, muted announcements that yes another album really was on the way, that album, 2016's *Wildflower*, was met with what can only be regarded as extraordinary praise for a band that had more or less eased itself into something that strongly resembled an early retirement. From 2016 to 2020, the band went on a comparative productivity binge. They released a double disc twentieth-anniversary edition of *Since I Left You* in June 2020, replete with sixteen new mixes. Another new album, *We Will Always Love You*, came out in December of that same year. All three resulted in a fairly substantial tranche of reflections, reconsiderations, and revisions of the status of *Since I Left You*.

The Greatness Attributed to Pop

There are a few things to understand about the particular historical trajectory of music writing since about 1985 or so that can help us account for this unusual career arc. First, the entire shape, scope, and purpose of how popular music is rendered into that elusive thing that exists just beyond the sum of its actual parts called "greatness" has changed in the last several decades. From the early to mid-1980s, the practice of applying the constellation of qualities said to constitute greatness started to radically expand. Instead of being reserved for an elite class of those regarded as manifestly awesome, a much wider range of artists regarded as great began to be placed confidently in the canon (Fairchild, 2024). This should hardly be surprising. Artists such as Michael Jackson, Madonna, Elton John, Prince, and Whitney Houston amassed audiences of unprecedented size and profitability. Dozens more artists have followed them across all main traditions of popular music practice into 1990s. Why wouldn't assignations of greatness follow what we can only define as extraordinary commercial dominance? Second, the specific, and by far the most common, form of greatness that is used to explain the extraordinary success of the top tier of profitable musicians has hardened into a clear and very nearly universal form. I've called it the rock imaginary. Simply put, the rock imaginary is a doctrine whose legitimation demands that artists deemed as "great" be true to themselves, their art, and their publics. Their work must be regarded as an honestly felt and acquired reflection of their character, their feelings, and their sense of self. Their expression of this self in their art must meet the highest forms of emotional and intellectual expression. And they and their work must somehow transcend the everyday world most of us inhabit, ideally stretching out even beyond time itself (Fairchild, 2021; see also Fairchild, 2024). If you look at the standard story of *Since I Left You*, it hits all of these marks, repeatedly.

There have been years of debate about who gets to be great. While these debates are fairly marginal in the grand scheme of things, they are revealing. At the turn of the new century, there had been a general consensus in "serious" popular music writing, both academic and not, that "pop" music had long been deliberately excluded from the mainstream of our collective culture. The advocates of pop, dance music, R&B, and allied genres declared themselves to be "poptimists." They spread a jittery rhetoric of faux-radical proclamations that demanded that their nemesis, "rockism," be stripped of its power to determine musical greatness and value. Between about 2001 and 2010, it was. As a result of poptimist agitations, we can now find "the same pretensions to aesthetic universality, artistic seriousness, and transcendent importance" in poptimism as we once found in rockism. In short, the rock imaginary became a dominant system of value for a lot more than rock (Fairchild, 2021: 180; see also Fairchild, 2024).

But it wasn't just the doctrine of what counts as acceptable forms of superlative musical expression that had changed. The ways in which this doctrine was produced had changed as well. Chief among these changes was the relationship between the artist and those writing about them. Since the mid-1980s, music writers have been subjected to far more exacting media management techniques by media corporations, record labels, press officers, and PR teams than ever before. The industry's main agenda has been to ration access to artists and more tightly control the content of interviews. Given that music writers are increasingly employed as freelancers or employed on short-term contracts, the balance of power between artists and journalists swung significantly toward artists and their handlers, that is, their managers and the media corporations that own their work (Forde, 2006, 2001; Hope, 2015).

The relationship between the writer and the musician is, overarchingly, a relationship between a publication and a record label, or more exactly, between what are almost always subsidiary appendages of powerful media conglomerates. As a result, institutionalized PR is the "primary definer" of the encounter between musician and journalist. Publicists, either working in-house at a record label or directly for the artist, have increasingly acted as interlocuters between the media and musicians. Access is doled out to approved writers who are one small part of larger more complex relationships of "mutual dependency" (Forde, 2006: 288). This dependency has produced what one journalist called an "economy of worship" in celebrity journalism (Hope, 2015).

This economy of worship is structurally enforced. Since the overwhelming digitalization of most forms of journalism, arts criticism and journalism have been increasingly packaged as adjuncts to products being written about. In other words, it has simply not been a problem for what used to be called "conflicts of interest" to be rebranded as "synergies." Media corporations are now able to direct and shape the writing about their own products to an unprecedented degree (Herrman, 2015; Paoletta, 2019). As such, a publication's survival is no longer based only on deriving revenue from the symbiotic tension between artist and critic that saw advertising rates driven by sales and subscriptions. Instead, economic sustainability turns on a very different set of tools used to measure and assess the economic value of the ways in which a readership might drive revenue by increasing their "engagement" (see Fairchild, 2024).

Pitchfork is widely regarded to have been "on the front lines of this boundary-pushing reconfiguration of music criticism and consumption" (Enis, 2020). A remarkable summary of the publication's first perfect 10.0 review tells us a lot about these changes. The review was for Radiohead's *Kid A*. *Pitchfork* regarded the reviews as part of an "extremely calculated" product rollout. The editor "had been building toward the release by stacking every section on the website with *Kid A* content, and he even reached out to Radiohead fan sites to let them know they were giving it a 10/10 so they could share the link." Given that the album was released just on the crest of a breaking wave that gradually pushed music consumption into the immediacy of illegal downloads and later, streaming, as opposed to the slight lag of physical formats, people could experience part or all of an album right away, usually without reading reviews beforehand. As such, the manipulations *Pitchfork* performed to drive traffic were duly innovative. The recounting of this story was blunt. The success of the *Kid A* review was dependent on the fact that the reviewer "managed to capture the historical awe of that moment with some of the most flamboyantly earnest, absurdly effusive, and borderline nonsensical bits of prose to ever be published in a legitimate music publication" (Enis, 2020). As we will see, there is little question that The Avalanches were the objects of a great many such effusions in 2001, 2016, and 2020.

To put it simply, when The Avalanches returned, they found the world of music writing to be even more amenable to them than the one they had enjoyed two decades earlier. This was not simply because the band were now so much better at their craft or that so many more people had finally "come around" to them or that "their" kind of music had taken over the world, or any other such mystical imaginings. It was because the way music was now rendered meaningful and valuable for most of us was very different than it was in 2001. The band's newly attributed greatness wasn't just simply waiting for them all that time, buried in the layers of painstakingly manipulated sound. It was the evolved means to bestow that greatness that reanimated this album. And we can see its initial kaleidoscopic expressions right from the start. While the first raptures of the reception of this album began in Australia, the canonization of *Since I Left You* really began in the UK.

The First Blush of Love Is Always the Most Memorable

It is instructive to compare the first round of Australian reviews to the genuine frenzy that awaited the band in the UK. The first Australian news stories about *Since I Left You* from October 2001 simply described "an ambitious concept album" (Duffy, 2000: 46). The band were described as "Melbourne underground heroes" who had produced an "unconventional" album and were touring Australia's east coast with "messed-up samples, disco stylings, pop enthusiasm, boundless energy and shambolic live sets" (Maksimovic, 2000: 37). About a month later, the band was charmingly described as "purveyors of a good-time musical jumbalaya incorporating R&B, soul, obscure television samples, jazz, lounge, hip-hop, electronica, classical and strings and flutes that sound as though they've been purloined from Fantasy Island or The Love Boat." In a little factoid that would become a staple of Avalanches lore, it was noted that "Madonna's label Maverick has expressed interest in The Avalanches after keeping track of the early EPs" and later "made history by allowing the band to sample the bassline from her song Holiday." They were "the first act ever allowed the privilege of legally taking a chunk from any Madonna product." The article then portentously noted that the band was also "about to become the subject of a five-page feature in Britain's influential magazine The Face" (Holmes, 2000:12).

Somewhat humorously, the early returns were not uniformly positive. The local Melbourne newspaper *The Age* briefly hosted an über-hip, oh-so-knowing column called "Culture Club" around that time, devoted to the goings-on at their city's nightclubs and in the dance music scene. In its edition of November 24, the authors sniffed that "the hiphop [*sic*] and beats act the Avalanches are now riding the coat-tails of their turntablist, Dexter, who's a household name among British DJ cognoscenti." Strangely, one member of that exalted group of tastemakers gave the single "Frontier Psychiatrist" "the dance industry's highest reviewing accolade: a score of five dancing men." They were apparently "[i]gnoring the tune's derivative cut-and-paste qualities" (Mast and Maunder, 2000:13).

The first major profile of the band also appeared in Melbourne's *The Age* newspaper the next week. The article was primarily about the hype that had been created around the band. They were said to have "come a long way from scouring second-hand record shops around Brunswick and Fitzroy and buying albums through the Trading Post." Ominously, the author relayed to his readers the fact that the buzz around the band in Australia "was merely a rumble compared to the excitement in London since a limited-edition party tape compilation and a bootleg of their debut album" had magically appeared (Donovan and Carew, 2000:12).

Two weeks later a review of the now-released album told us how it was "impossible not to fall for the slinky, shimmering pop of the title track, which mixes a warm, '60s lounge feel with some flute action and cruising funk. A generous slab of Madonna's Holiday follows, while Radio is stunning, steered by funky samples and random vocals." The album moved seamlessly forward, "plundering everything from tender ballads to hard-edged electro, proving that world-class music can come from our backyard." The band's "post-modern disco-pop amalgam from rubbish '50s rejects and saccharine '60s pap" had attracted famous fans from international musical firmament, including the aforementioned Queen of Pop as well as a Beastie Boys producer and the mysterious legend Van Dyke Parks (Adams, 2000: 6). A few consensus themes persisted in the writing about the album, especially the unconventional nature of the music as well as the painstaking labor that had produced it. Unsurprisingly, the British music press would greatly intensify these themes in their own manufactured hysteria.

The initial UK release in April 2001 had a slightly different set of priorities. The first was to note the album's "freshness." As London's *The Times* told its readers, "plagiarism and predictability are at a weary, all-time high" in dance music. "Thankfully," they sighed in relief, "there is some freshness on the horizon with the debut release from the Avalanches." As with many UK publications, geography mattered, a lot. The band "originate from Australia and their relative cultural isolation means that they have avoided paying lip service to American or British trends" (Aston, 2001: 10). Another familiar theme in this kind of writing is to note the hype as if one is simply observing it from afar:

> Here's how to go about creating the year's most talked about album. First, aim to produce a life-affirming, flowing piece of work in the tradition of Marvin Gaye's What's Goin' On, or those classic, thematically driven Stevie Wonder albums. Next, don't bother writing any original material—you can steal what you need by sampling other people's music. Then, once you have amassed a formidable second-hand record collection and developed unimpeachable taste (vintage soul, Crosby, Stills & Nash, ELO, Nina Simone), you can begin the painstaking task of constructing your opus. Well, it worked for the Avalanches.
>
> (Shepherd, 2001: 8)

Calling the band a "balearic Beach Boys," readers were told that "the growing army of admirers who have fallen for their charming debut" have done so "because it is such a sonic joy" (Shepherd, 2001: 8). Please note the subtle nod to the presumed tastemaking, trendsetting intent of the band.

One of the most verbose and persistent champions of the album was music critic Simon Reynolds. His technique, hardly unique to him, was to speak to the reader in the third person, again to act as if he was merely observing the hype he was helping stoke as if it were a distant phenomenon, akin to the transit of Venus or Haley's Comet:

> You're almost set up to be underwhelmed by this Australian outfit's debut. Amazingly, *Since I Left You* lives up to the hype.

> At the end, you feel dazed and bemused, partly because you're concussed by its tumultuous on-rush of non-stop brilliance, but also because it's hard to put your finger on why The Avalanches are so special, so different.

Reynolds concurs that it was "the group's delight at the sonic jetsam they've salvaged is palpable in every bar of the record" that set it apart (Reynolds, 2001).

The theme of freshness took on many shapes. One review noted that in "mediocre hands, sampling can make for dull, lazy music, but Melbourne cut-and-paste merchants the Avalanches are as accomplished in technique as they are rich in imagination" (Horan, 2001). Another reviewer thought that the album had "gelled into an eclectic, frenetic and never less than entertaining marathon of juicy beats and samples" and was as "amusing as it is refreshing and enjoyable" (Horan, 2001). One Irish writer imagined the freshness made the album a summer staple:

> [T]hose lazy, hazy, crazy days of summertime, complete with the customary scents and sounds of barbeques, cut grass and the hum of low-flying planes. Despite this seasonal utopia vibe, there's something missing, something not quite right as you soak up the sunshine, sipping your adequately chilled bottle of beer. Of course! You haven't had the sense to purchase "Since I Left You", the Avalanches picnic basket of musical treats.

Again noting that distance might add to their charms, the fact that they were from Australia helped establish the band as "the unlikely champions of a musical echelon that's tiring of superstar DJs and unimaginative revisionism" (Gleeson, 2001).

In these many reflections and responses, a somewhat unwitting and back and forth of hemispheric imaginings emerged. In an interview with *The Guardian*, Chater suggested that the album "couldn't have been made anywhere else. Growing up in Melbourne, the rest of the world seems like such an amazing, wonderful place. In your imagination a lot of these countries are just magical, they are so far away" (Barkham, 2001: 16). He later remembered that this initial flash of intense interest was "all a little bit surreal." He recalled that magazines he had grown up reading were now dispatching their writers halfway around the world to write about them. As he told Steve Bell:

> I also remember lots of Brits saying, this is just what they imagined life on the beach in Australia sounded like, you know, like just a big beach party. And we were like, kind of, well, we're from Melbourne and there's not really any great beaches and that's probably why we had come to make a record like this. But for us, it's funny because like we love like West Coast American, you know, music like Beach Boys and Crosby Stills and stuff like that. So for us, it was like always dreaming of another place. And it's funny that how for people in England that they thought it sounded like Australia.
>
> (Bell, 2021)

This theme, no doubt endemic to certain parts of the Northern Hemisphere, imagined the Australia that produced this album to be a perpetually sundrenched utopia. Some probably already knew that this was a climate from which Melbourne had been largely exempted.

The Face, invited along on a record company schmooze cruise in December 2000, began its profile on this note, quoting the first recognizable sample on the album:

> Have a drink. Welcome to paradise! Welcome, indeed to Australia. Bathed in dazzling December sunshine, 300 of Melbourne's premier party people up the gangplank of the Victoria Star, a pleasure boat moored in Victoria harbour. It might be Sunday afternoon, but everyone here is in their best Friday- night flash: bovs in boxfresh trainers, girls in tottering heels. They've come to celebrate the launch of the debut album by Australian group The Avalanches. It's a record largely without precedent … that you will come to love over the next few months.
>
> (Warren, 2001: 158)

This article, a full feature about a mostly unknown band a long, long way away, was the first of several such lengthy profiles to be published between March and October 2001. The others appeared in the aggressively underground electronic music publication *Jockey Slut*, the third in the preciously brand-conscious *Q* magazine, and the fourth in the conspicuously hedonic dance music magazine *Muzik*. In sum, they brought this multiyear interest in the band to a peak that it would not reach again until 2016.

Interestingly, despite their contrasting status and style, *Jockey Slut* reproduced both the themes and intensity of descriptive interest *The Face* had, this time from two of Australia's actual "paradises": the Gold Coast and Byron Bay. The author's interest in their music took a slightly more expansive tone, noting that their show "had weaved its way through theremin abuse, punk rock, turntablism and bursts of Cyndi Lauper," and the album itself, while flirting with being a "kitchen sink mess," instead was made to cohere "through sheer pop savvy … From lump-throatening melancholic moments, like the beautiful title track, through the cartoon goonery of the funky 'Frontier Psychiatrist' and the mutant coffee table touches of the outro, it rocks against the orthodox" (Burgess, 2001).

Q's feature was by far the shortest, but kept to the script in an extremely concise way. Under a picture of the band lounging at the same waterfront *The Face* described, the article told its readers of a "sophisticated collage of disco, pop, psychedelia, hip hop, Madonna and assorted junk shop exotica, it took a full two years to construct but nevertheless remains playful, charming and thoroughly upbeat" (Lynskey, 2001: 34). Its four-star review at the back of the magazine explained that the album was great because of its, well, freshness. It presented "an outrageous. loony-tunes landscape" that "finally fulfils sampling's original promise of generating fabulous new sounds from skillfully lifted bits of existing tracks. Not for them the usual round of drum loops and dialogue nicked from anger management tapes" (Kone, 2001: 102).

Muzik's profile kept up with the publication's abiding loyalty to sex, drugs, and dance music. Each page featured a full background photo of each member of the band seemingly leaping through a dimly lit space. The writer stoked the sleaze with copious references to "willy waving," "genital exposure," "aural foreplay," and enormous pull quotes about "getting a bit of arse." Eventually, we are treated to a familiar description of the band's live and recorded work, the former being an "hour long fusillade of musical cutups, sonic snippets" and the album being a "colourful patchwork of insouciant pop melodies, breezy disco house, raw hip hop, insane humour and heart-wrenching melancholy, wrung from literally hundreds of sample snippets, the band's debut album is a truly stoic and visionary work" (Sullivan, 2001: 61, 64).

The Love Comes Home

The response in Australia to all of the attention the band were getting overseas was interesting. The story of their overseas success was incorporated into the overall narrative of the band fairly early on. Again, the tone was almost entirely observational. In January 2001, one writer explained that "The Avalanches are a textbook example of how landslides happen. After two years teetering on major success, locally and overseas, there were only subtle indications of what the group was going to unleash" (Duffy, 2001: 44). Another surmised that their success was inevitable. Electronic music had a "do- it-yourself ethos, [a] liberating portability, [and] hypnotic rhythms" that are "replacing what we once knew as 'live' music and what we are seeing take its place is not merely the next phase of rock music but something new" (Shanahan, 2001: O1). A month later this same writer, now a genuine champion of the band, was asking his readership, "Just how big can The Avalanches become?" He reported back that the band's second single, the title track, had "just made it on to Britain's Radio 1, and in the lead-up to the European release of the album, they've been showcased in a four-page special in *The Face* magazine; are on the cover of next month's *Jockey Slut*; are favorites of British dance mag 7 (who called DJ Dexta the first exciting turntablist of the millennium); and have upcoming features in *Q* and *NME*" (Donovan, 2001b:5). He described that single "as so timeless and rootless that few would guess it was made by a Melbourne electronic hiphop [*sic*] band in 2000" (Donovan, 2001a:7).

That same month, another report reached the antipodes, regaling the locals with stories of their local lads done good. The scene was "one of London's coolest clubs, the Social, the venue in which the Chemical Brothers cut their turntable teeth a few years back." The scene's "'next big things' are spinning tunes for London's in-crowd." Their various subterranean mixes had "been furiously circulating for more than a year in parts of the UK music scene, with all the right people gushing all the right compliments over the mixture of samples, melodies and fun." In fact, the interest had been "so intense" that "a journalist from *The Face* flew to Melbourne last year to cover the album's hometown launch, resulting in a four-page spread in the notoriously hip magazine." Beyond that, the band had "also graced everything from DJ mag Jockey Slut to NME, while their first UK single, Since I Left You, has been all over Radio One (the UK's biggest network). The gossip from "British music industry insiders" about "the single means it might crashland in the UK Top 10" (Adams, 2001:40). By the end of the year, the story was set. "A group of mates from Brunswick" had taken a "well-worn path of local musicians between Australian garages and London clubs." They did so "in the footsteps of such legends as The Saints, Nick Cave's band The Birthday Party, Dave Graney, the Triffids and the Go Betweens." However, "while many of those bands ended up in decrepit squats … The Avalanches were quickly embraced by Britain's thriving dance music scene":

> The British music press, which can create or ruin a band with hype overnight, are always on the lookout for new sounds, especially in the dance scene, which evolves more quickly than traditional rock and pop music. The Avalanches—virtually unknown outside their home-ground hip-hop community—went on to sell 140,000 copies of their debut album *Since I Left You* in Britain, and it is still in the charts there six months after its release.
>
> (Donovan, 2001c:13)

In short, while the band were "virtually anonymous to most mainstream Australian record buyers," they were still "being hailed as the musical find of the year by critics here, in the US and the UK" (Scatena, 2001:31). Amazingly, "the sample-happy Melbourne collective of punk-band escapees and old vinyl aficionados into one of the most talked about bands on the planet" (Mengel, 2001: M08).

The journey from here to a gratefully bestowed and permanently possessed greatness, while long, seems straightforward at least. There were subtle hints of it very early. Unsurprisingly, one of the earliest reviews was from *Pitchfork*. The tone was both capital "S" serious and underhandedly hip. The author tried to balance some fairly grand-sounding summaries of a presumed cultural zeitgeist with an underground sensibility:

> Sure, nobody bats an eye when copyright law takes some money out of the shiny, rhinestone-encrusted pockets of Rob Van Winkle or Puff Daddy, but as soon as lawsuits trip up avant-hoodlums like John Oswald of Plunderphonics fame, the concept of thievery-as-art becomes a hot topic, and the line between sampling and stealing becomes fiercely contended.

He carefully pointed out what he called "obvious sonic mismatches" and the kind of bizarre pairing of classic soul with futuristic sounds that he felt defined "a substantial part of Avalanches magic." He then trotted out his skills at aural observation of the new and inventive:

> And while many of these songs rely heavily on the repetition of beats and samples, no single part of the record is allowed to stagnate … a sample transposed up or down a few steps, a beat chopped up into little pieces and seamlessly

restructured, an unexpected vocal sample popping up out of nowhere before being swallowed up by the massive sound the Avalanches have concocted.

His summary paragraph is almost uncanny in its conformity to the narrative that would follow in the years to come:

> The Avalanches have essentially brought hundreds of slabs of inanimate vinyl to life. Though it was no doubt meticulously constructed, this is an album brimming with spontaneity, joy, sadness, humor, reflection, and general human-ness. With its high fun factor and subtle traces of deeper emotion, Since I Left You is the perfect record for the party, and for the period of regret and recovery after the party.
>
> (LeMay, 1999)

A review of a live show by The Avalanches in London captures this ethos more directly. The band had made a form of music that "captured the non-sequiturial (il)logic of dreams—the sudden shape-shifting between the everyday and the bizarre." Their work:

> marked the welcome return to pop's palette of sheer joy in a year dominated by navel-gazing minstrels and discordant complaint rockers, a record which makes music sound the way it sounded coming out of Medium-Wave car radios on childhood holidays, drifting in and out of your consciousness.
>
> (Price, 2001:11)

Admission into the Canon

The above passages mostly capture the content of the revival and canonization of Since I Left You some two decades later.

The most important thing to understand about the tide of writing produced about The Avalanches from 2016 onward is the extent to which it dwarfs both in scale and scope the collected output found from 2000 to 2002. The reason for this is the transformation of the relationship between writer, artist, and reader noted earlier. If audience "engagement" is measured in all of the data produced and harvested by clicks and visits, then more writing equals more engagement. The writer Richard Seymour has pithily summarized writing in the age of social media. Social media "more often works by making us speak, coaxing our confessions, our testimonies, our cries from the heart, out of us." The "Twittering Machine," as he calls it, "will goad us." The machine "is coercive, harnessed to ceaseless production." He argues that the "cathartic effect of writing, reacting to stimulus, can be a way of filling the void with endless monetizable chatter" (Seymour, 2019: 204).

This chatter was all the more productive because of the nature of the music itself. *Since I Left You* had a deep and specific kind of ambiguity to it that somehow managed to capture a particular way of experiencing music. It is both distant and intimate at the same time, sometimes floating like a half-remembered dream, at other times demanding a certain visceral head-nodding, hip-sliding bodily groove. In fact, it was so formless yet so enervating that a lot of people simply imprinted their fantasies onto it, fantasies that could never really be contradicted.

Chater reflected on this years later in his conversation with journalist Steve Bell. He described "this magical moment where we found our own place in the musical universe and we're like, we're going to make a record that sounds like a lost transmission. And it doesn't have to work on the dance floor, it can, but it doesn't have to." Importantly, they made "a conscious decision to remove ourselves from the record." He continues:

> We didn't play any instruments. We didn't sing or add any vocals like we had previously ... It just felt like a beautiful transmission floating in from elsewhere. And when we hit upon that sort of sound ... And that was it. So it's just like a wonderful thing to experience actually when everything sort of comes together and you're in this beautiful state of flow. And a record like that just comes pouring out.
>
> (Bell, 2021)

It was this absence of presence, still a fairly novel quality in 2000, that can help account for the specific ways in which this album was designated "great." An early reflection in *The Guardian* on the legacy of the album, from 2011, told us that "*Since I Left You* is not just a nostalgic fantasy voyage, it's an album about the evocative power of music, and how just a fragment of it has the ability to open up whole new vistas of the imagination" (Richards, 2011). Several years later, after *Wildflower* had appeared, another writer from the same publication told us that *Since I Left You* had "spawned both a string of hit singles and a succession of reviews that boggled over the painstaking work and imagination that must have gone into making it: more than 3,500 samples meticulously stitched together into a seamless hour of music" (Petridis, 2016). That first album, another writer explained, was "[c]rafted from a dreamy tapestry of mostly obscure samples." It was "peculiar in that, unlike most sample-based albums, it wasn't striving to reflect its creators' personal politics—it wasn't showing off. It sought to reflect something that didn't previously exist" (Ediriwira, 2016). That elusive something, we were told in 2016, had set itself to "capturing the wide-eyed, mucking-about-on-school-holidays- and-eating-icypoles-in-a-strange-coastal-town mood of the first record, the sweet and sour seesaw of the human condition." Chater agreed, explaining that "There's something about the human voice. I often think about every radio station playing all at once and every singer from every era, all these radio transmissions floating into outer space. From John Lennon to Elvis, they're all floating around up there in the ether" (Cahill, 2016).

These themes persisted for years, growing ever more mystical with time. The album, it was said, "floats through the liminal space between the crate-pillaging hip-hop visionaries like the Dust Brothers and Prince Paul were spearheading around the turn of the '90s and the MP3 orgy overseen by festival-slaying mash-up king Girl Talk." This space produced an effect that was "like being swept away into a fantastical world in the middle of the night, where the beachfront dance parties are tinged with melancholy and the drowsier you get, the more clarity you attain." The "endless parade of sounds stitched together seamlessly" produced "a wistful calm hangs over everything, a warm, woozy nostalgia for a moment you're not sure ever really existed" (Deville, 2020). The album had an uncanny "sense of elusiveness," according to another essay, existing as "something forever slightly out of reach, of ecstasy so nearly grasped. It is redolent of longing, but also of the pleasures of the quest." It provided the sense of "a world imagined through music, infuses the whole album" (Bennun, 2020).

The broadest assessments saw something very, very special and historically overwhelming. Said one, "The Avalanches' *Since I Left You* is a secluded spot out of time and space, a moment made in the unlikely intersections of culture and craft. An experience greater than the sum of its parts, though that sum is formidable all the same" (Herbert, 2021). Another reported that the music had "no date stamp on the sounds, the feel or the result. This still sounds gorgeous and incredibly detailed in the ear, sparkling in the brain, and revealing, in its consistent reality, the way pleasure and the abstract can be given equal weight with the mechanical and practical" (Zuel, 2021).

These effusive missives of unrestrained praise nearly all speak of the honest labor of the musicians, of a masterful work that reached the highest forms of emotional and intellectual expression imaginable, one that somehow transcended the everyday world in which it was made, stretching out beyond time itself. In the next and final chapter, we will try to cut through some of this otherworldly prose and take a close look at the music that produced such a response.

5 The Aesthetics of *Since I Left You*

In the previous chapters I suggested that one of the foundational gestures of *Since I Left You* was an attempt to forge a coherence out of the often intimidating disorder of the world. In this chapter, we will look at the techniques used to do this and the experience of the results. To do this, we need to understand the musical world into which The Avalanches were inserted and made use of to present their work. To do this we need to start with a clear understanding of a few terms that will help us make sense of this album. These are: *aesthetics*, *medium*, and *materials*.

Often, people write about sampling as an "aesthetic" but this is not quite right. Sampling is a set of compositional techniques. Calling sampling an "aesthetic" tends to level out all works that use this compositional technique in ways that prevent us from understanding the distinctions between them. In order to understand the "aesthetic" of a sampled-based work, we also need to understand in a general sense how that piece of music is made socially sensible and comprehensible as music. Therefore, the "aesthetics" of a work that uses the techniques of sampling is made up of something more than just these particular techniques. The aesthetics of such a work include not only the musical materials used to make it but also the skills and techniques that have been imposed on those materials. But it doesn't stop there. It also includes the broad consensus of the meanings of these worked-on materials and the forms of social connection and understanding produced within relevant social worlds about that work. Most often, such understandings are produced by people closest to the kind of work being made and whose interpretations can claim a decent amount of legitimacy.

As I argued some time ago, a defining feature of sample-based music is that it "exhibits particular kinds of musical fidelity" between the recordings that were sampled and the work that has been constructed from them. Further, the relationships between the source materials and completed work are used by musicians to "create various kinds of consonance and dissonance between source texts and the new works derived from them." As a result, the new work is "held together by particular kinds of aesthetic legitimacy, or the ways in which the relationship between new works and older works within this particular tradition of practice is understood and accepted" (Fairchild, 2014: 63–4). This means that the social world into which this album was inserted played a key role in conferring legitimacy on it because it was recognized as part of a specific tradition of practice that people already implicitly recognized as such. This happened through "the play of recognition between producers and audiences produced by new uses of previously existing recorded music" (Fairchild, 2014: 63–4).

I drew this claim from the work of Theodore Gracyk, whose summation of the concept of the medium and materials of popular music is central to my understanding of *Since I Left You*. Gracyk draws on a range of work in the philosophy of art and aesthetics to explain how we can understand the particular ways in which an artistic medium acts as "a mode of organizing perception and of unpacking meanings" (Gracyk, 1996: 69). He notes how the philosopher Timothy Binkley's definition of a medium is helpful because Binkley does not simply focus on the materials with which an artist works, whether these are paint or words or sounds, but also on the conventions which define how those materials and the aesthetic qualities we attribute to them are mediated. Gracyk explains that to "understand a medium is to know which qualities are relevant to something's counting as a specific work." This includes how we know what qualities are important to a work and how we learn how to experience them (Gracyk, 1996: 69–70). These understandings are often unstated or inchoate. Very often we "just know" what they are and what they mean. However, instead of simply being told what to think or experience, it is the *practice* of artists that most directly guides us. That is, artists work with their materials in ways that are characteristic of their tradition of musical practice. As Gracyk says, for music, "the medium is a range of allowable sounds together with principles for structuring those sounds" (Gracyk, 1996:71). He concludes:

> The upshot is that the audience's reception of art—high or low—requires an understanding of how aesthetic qualities and meanings emerge from the materials. We read works against a horizon of potentialities and limitations that artists explore in materials.
>
> (Gracyk, 1996:72)

If we listen closely and make use of the wealth of materials that have been produced about this album, we can use these ideas to understand it in a very detailed way.

We should note a fairly simple fact before we get too far along: the "medium" in which this album has circulated has changed dramatically since the album was produced. The initial medium was made in part from equipment whose capabilities were soon-to-be obsolete. It moved around the world on things like CDs and vinyl records. It was brought to the audience's attention through radio programs, news and magazine articles, music videos broadcast on television, and underground mixes and bootlegs. While all of these things continue to exist, most are now much closer to historical curiosities than anything like a cutting edge. Importantly, the effectiveness of this initial medium faded naturally, so to speak. By the time its constituent elements were replaced, stand-alone samplers by DAWs, individual components by laptops, CDs by streaming platforms, and so-called legacy media by social media, The Avalanches were nearing a decade in semi-retirement. When they reemerged, a greatly evolved medium took up their work and ran with it and did so in new ways. However, when they did come back, the long-surpassed tools and techniques used to make the album were a primary topic of interest and analysis. This is because what these musicians actually did mattered and still does. So let's start there.

One Hour of Sampled Sunshine

The album consists of eighteen seamlessly blended tracks that form a complete hour-long whole. The album's continuous flow and seamless integration of a multitude of source materials on both the macro scale and the micro defines it more than any other quality. The second crucial quality of the album feeds into this: layering. The samples are all meticulously arranged in relation to one another in multiple, continuously evolving layers that often mirror or even mimic the way different parts of an ensemble are layered in typical recordings. One of the reasons this is so important is the sheer volume of samples and the relative anonymity of the vast majority of them. One of the key points of lore about the album is that nobody, not even the band, really knows exactly how many samples were actually used. At different times, the numbers have ranged from around 900 to more than 3000. No one can say how many were used because of the way so many were used. The vast majority are impossible to identify. They consist of tiny moments of sound taken from their sources and reformed completely out of context. These instants of recorded sound are used as if they were acoustic instruments, such as drums, cymbals, guitars, strings, flutes, and horns. Far fewer in number, but of far greater prominence, were the riffs and beats from well-known songs, the sample of Madonna's "Holiday" being the most renowned.

The first thing to think about compositionally is the identification of samples which is dependent on finding source materials. One of the most entertaining aspects of the album is not simply the huge numbers of samples but their confounding diversity. The samples don't just come from old vinyl records but also from television shows and films. And remember, this was well before YouTube and the rest of the internet offered musicians endless aural riches to sample. Chater told *Pitchfork* that they used to have to go out and get VHS tapes of films from video stores and treat them like old records. This is how they found their famous horse sample used in "Stay Another Season" and "Frontier Psychiatrist" ("The Avalanches Break Down ...," 2021).

Sampling is very plainly a practice shaped by very specific kinds of listening, skills which are in turn dependent on a whole host of subtle musical practices some of which can be very idiosyncratic. Chater told journalist Steve Bell that his listening practices were based on "the joy of discovery and even on some strange old record that I couldn't listen to all the way through, there's just these little beautiful moments" (Bell,

2021). Despite having been sampling records for decades, he still couldn't quite articulate how the process works: "I can be listening to a record one day and be in a certain mood and not really hear any samples on it and then you know six months later I'm in a completely different mood one morning and the sun's coming through the window and I'm just hearing these beautiful moments all over the place." Despite this, he did note that they do "catalogue stuff," such as instrumental sounds or sonic textures, and file them away for later use, but they "try to keep it in the spirit of the moment and we're working from intuition, working from our heart" (Bell, 2021).

An important aspect of how the sampling was done for this album has to do with crate digging in Melbourne in the 1990s specifically. Tony Di Blasi explained to Bell that "Melbourne crate digging back then was so different" and that "in our rock shops here we had the weirdest stuff and ... we kind of had to make do with all that ... I feel like if we were you know in New York to make that record it would have sounded completely different" (Bell, 2021). Di Blasi explained that the endless stores of extremely inexpensive vinyl records readily available to them definitively shaped the sound of the album. It seems clear that what they found in their many, many trips to suburban op shops and junk stores was a strange panoply of forgotten, rejected, or lost records. Rather than what Di Blasi described as all the "cool" and "amazing" music people found to sample elsewhere, in Melbourne it seemed to him that "we just didn't have that here. You just didn't come across it and if people had that music they [would] keep it" (Bell, 2021).

The other thing that both Chater and Di Blasi explained was the very specific ways in which what we now see as the rigid limitations of their sampling equipment shaped the album. Di Blasi said that the samplers they used "couldn't fit that much music" onto them so "you ... have a beat and a couple samples." Chater thought that how they worked then was

> a completely different way of working to how you work now, where ... you see every sample laid out on your laptop in front of you. So yeah, there's something about them that had a really particular sound and a really beautiful sort of crunchy sound. And I just became incredibly good at just using that one piece of equipment.

He regarded the limitations to be "a really good thing. The samplers could only hold so much audio and they only had so much memory. ... Basically, I would just fill one and that's as much sound as I could load at one time. So that would be a song and that's when a song was finished" (Bell, 2021).

The skilled manipulation and laborious organization of the samples is clearly what makes them so effective. All of the samples were manipulated across all the main parameters of musical sound—pitch, tone, texture, duration, and rhythm—usually exhibiting manipulations of most or all of these at once. The purpose of these manipulations was to smooth them all into a seamless whole, that is, organizing disparate musical gestures and ordinary sounds into a common key, tempo, and structure. This is what catches your ear as soon as you start listening.[1] The first track on the album, the title

---

[1] I have used a few key sources that identified most of the clearly audible source material for this album. The most useful was an explainer produced by the "moonwalker" YouTube channel (https://www.youtube.com/watch?v=31gTur14Hbc), a link to a still-extant Google doc posted by moonwalker, and a video produced by the "Bandstand" productions YouTube channel which seems to have also been produced by whoever produced the moonwalker channel (https://www.youtube.com/watch?v=MFEZiMyfSYI).

track, uses a range of aurally distinct and prominent samples to produce what amounts to a whole new song, complete with distinct sections that appear consistently throughout the duration of the track.[2] Each section has one or two samples that are the main feature of that section. The track begins with the sounds of a group of voices laughing and talking in the background.[3] A brief snippet of acoustic jazz guitar enters in the front of the mix,[4] and then a sample of light woodwinds and strings[5] subtly enters underneath to guide us smoothly to the entry of the drums,[6] with a vocal quartet vamping back and forth between two major chords.[7] Just over ten seconds in, the track is grooving in a mid-tempo soul sound and feel, syncopated and easy.

Listening carefully, we can hear that this "verse" has two sections. The first sits on the two-chord vamp which continually lands on the tonic. The second sits on a similar two-chord figure that moves between two chords higher up the scale. Each pattern is repeated one after the other several times. This second part is unstable as neither chord is the tonic and it is constantly pushing us back to the main figure which, happily enough, always arrives with the lines "since I met you, I've found a world so new" attached to it.[8] As the track moves forward, we can hear at least half a dozen prominent samples

---

[2] In Figure 2, I have used black arrows to note the major section changes in each of the first four tracks.

[3] "Daddy Rich" by Rose Royce (1976).

[4] "Anema E Core" by Tony Mottola (1962).

[5] "Younger Than Springtime" by Charles Davis (1959).

[6] "Take Off the Make Up" by Lamont Dozier (1973).

[7] "The Sky's the Limit" by The Duprees (1968).

[8] It should be noted that the actual phrase from the original source is "since I met you" and that has not been changed.

move around this core, appearing and disappearing into the imaginary ether produced by the track. These new sounds mark new sections, with each taking the aural lead in their respective sections. Right from the start we can hear how the samples are used in interlocking layers to create a continually evolving soundscape that only changes in moments that are carefully built up, approached, and realized. All of this creates a deeply anchored and abiding continuity throughout the album.

The continuity is not only aural but thematic and motivic as well. We hear this in the second track "Stay Another Season," as it builds on the "party" theme of the title track. Famously, the title track uses a vocal sample from the justly forgotten film *Club Med* from 1986, in which one of the hosts at a Mediterranean resort welcomes arriving guests with the line "Welcome to paradise." This sets in train what many commentators have cited as the "party" atmosphere of the album. "Stay Another Season" builds on this by using the bass, percussion, and rhythm guitar lines from Madonna's "Holiday" for about the first fifty seconds of the track. Contributing to this is a rich, quilted background pattern of voices, some in crowds, some addressing crowds, others being sung voices that have been chopped and looped. This works in tandem with "Holiday." As happens throughout the album, things change after all of this coheres for about a minute. The material from "Holiday" is eased out of the mix and is replaced by about ten seconds of carefully synced congas, drums, and handclaps,[9] again with ancillary sounds swirling around it. This then gives way to a new section in a minor key, expertly anticipated with a classical

---

[9] "Don't Leave Me (Instrumental)" by Holland-Dozier (1972).

violin passage[10] that somehow manages to lead us to a minor key samba pattern played on an electric piano.[11] The by-now familiar voice singing "Since I met you ..." has continued subtly throughout. This repeated splash of continuity is striking as the material surrounding it has just effected the album's first substantial (and nearly total) mood change at just about the five-minute mark. After about forty seconds of this, the texture around the samba begins to thin out and everything fades until a siren takes the foreground to signal the start of the next track called "Radio."

"Radio" begins as the siren at the end of "Stay Another Season" fades. A new rhythm section gradually enters far in the background, emerging from behind the siren. It gradually becomes full at about fifteen seconds into the new track. Notably, the first three tracks of the album have maintained the same tempo and stayed in the same key which clearly goes a long way to forming them into a unified block. The drum tracks of "Radio" are allied with various muted exhortations that readily recall the sounds of late 1980s "party" music.[12] This is enhanced by what sounds like someone noodling in the lower registers of something like a keytar. The vocals at this point are a woman's voice intoning the phrase "Sending those signals" over and over again.[13] At about 1.45 into the track another female vocal enters, singing "sometimes you don't understand" in a constrained three-note melodic loop.[14] The incorporation

---

[10] Bruch's Violin Concerto in G Minor performed by Jascha Heifetz (1964).

[11] "Cinnamon and Clove" by Sergio Mendes and Brazil 66 (1967).

[12] "So Into You" by Atlanta Rhythm Section (1976) and "Fat City Strut" by Mandrill (1973).

[13] Interview with Laurie Anderson from the film soundtrack to *Home of the Brave* (1986).

[14] "One Must Cry" by The Main Attraction (1967).

of the latter in particular, with the keytar-sounding line, is truly uncanny. It is impossible to hear the historical distance between the two original sources. Throughout most of the track, a fuzzy, scratchy background layer of sound persists as does an endless series of barely melodic bleeps and beeps. The track ends with another sample carefully deployed to overlap with the next track, a man fervently asking, "Can't you hear it?"[15]

The new track, "Two Hearts in 3/4 Time," briefly but sharply marks a pause in the unity of the first three tracks. The tempo is different, the rhythms are heavily syncopated, and the samples are far more aggressively manipulated than any of the previous ones. The first thirty seconds of the track are almost showy in the same way DJs from the DMC World DJ Championships often remake the entire rhythmic matrix of a familiar source track. The male voice continues his desperate intonation of the line "Can't you hear it?" surrounded by a one-off chime and a goofy horn taking about eleven seconds. Then, a sharp and syncopated sample of what sounds like a vertical cut of an entire track of another song, including male and female voices pinging around in a hocket with a guitar, underpinned by a bass line and accompanying silvery background percussion strikes, all stride across the soundscape very loudly.[16] The voices veer up a minor second here and back down below the starting note and then they all cut out abruptly after about fifteen seconds. They are replaced with a resonant electric piano line that almost mimics a distant fairground calliope, but somehow manages to sound weirdly tasteful.[17]

---

[15] "Rosemary" from the film soundtrack to *How to Succeed in Business without Really Trying* (1961).

[16] "With a Little Help from My Friends" by Tony Mottola (1968).

[17] "Rainbow Seven" by Neil Ardley (1976).

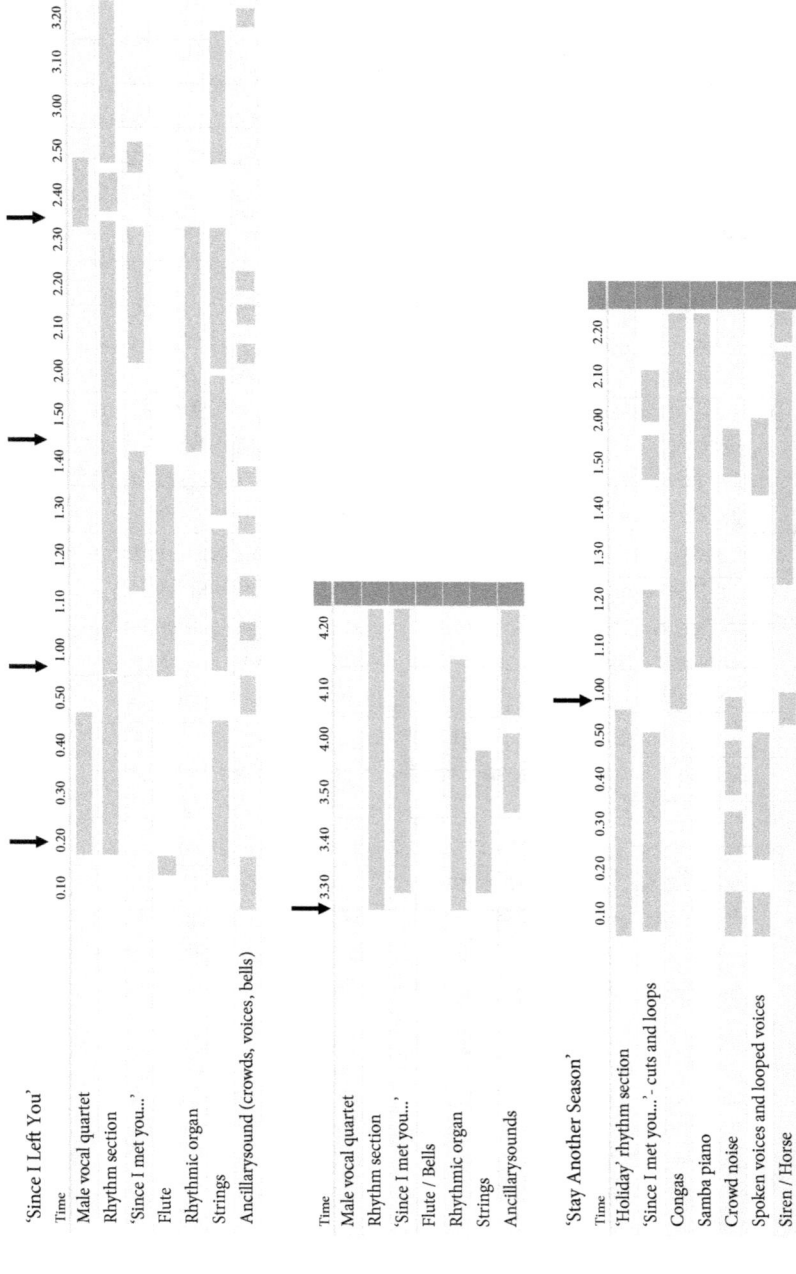

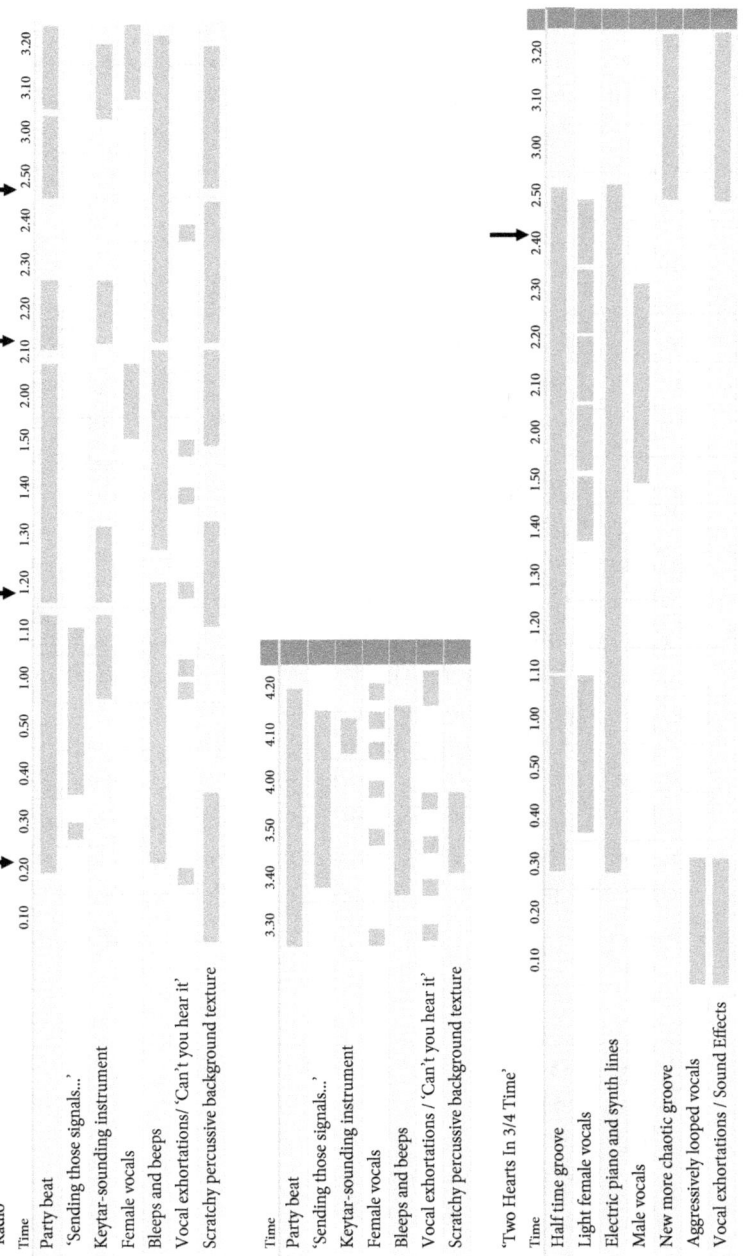

Figure 2 *Layering and timing of samples, Tracks 1–4,* Since I Left You.

We are back to most of the key attributes of the first three tracks in terms of tonal center and tempo. This is accompanied by a light, descending female vocal line.[18] The rhythm section eases everything along in a mid-tempo funk groove with all the low end removed, if such a thing can make sense. This part of the track has two strongly defined sections that each repeat. It lasts just over two minutes before it fades out, replaced by an entirely unrelated and far more busy bass and drum part[19] that scratches its way for well under a minute before it too fades into the distance. This section is much more aggressive and chaotic. It is here at 2.48 into "Two Hearts in 3/4 Time" that the first set definitively comes to an end. The track ends with a male voice intoning "avalanche rock, get" over and over.[20] Unsurprisingly, this leads us into the twenty-three second track entitled "Avalanche Rock." The vocals continue their chant over what sounds like an unholy cross between hotel lounge music and something from a late 1970s exploitation flick.[21] This is clearly a transition track leading us to a new section of the album defined by a new tempo, rhythm, and mood.

The first four tracks constitute what we might call the opening set of the album, with "Avalanche Rock" acting as a transition to a new set. In sum, the first act comprised one quarter of the total duration of the album. It set a pattern repeated throughout the rest of the tracks (see Figure 2). The

---

[18] "Yu Ma/Go Away Little Boy" by Marlena Shaw (1977).
[19] "Ghost Story" by John Cale (1970).
[20] "Glaciers of Ice" by Raekwon (1995).
[21] "Bang Bang" by Xavier Cugat (1966).

Set 1	"Since I Left You"	"Stay Another Season"	"Radio"	"Two Hearts In 3/4 Time"	Total Time
	(4.21)	(2.19)	(4.21)s	(3.25)	14.15
	"Avalanche Rock" (0.23)—Transition track				
Set 2	"Flight Tonight"	"Close To You"	"Diners Only"	"A Different Feeling"	
	(3.53)	(3.56)	(1.34)	(4.23) Change at 3.34	14.09
Set 3	"Electricity"	" Tonight May Have To Last Me All My Life"			
	(3.30)	(2.20)			6.50
Set 4	"Pablo's Cruise"		"Frontier Psychiatrist"		
	(0.52) Change at (0.36)		(4.48)		5.04
Set 5	"ETOH"	"Summer Crane"	"Little Journey"	"Live At Dominoes"	
	(5.04)	(4.39)	(1.36)	(5.39)	18.58
Coda	"Extra Kings"				
	(3.42)				3.42

Figure 3 Since I Left You *divided into five sets and a coda.*

album is clearly marked by sets, some of which correspond to the divisions between tracks, some of which don't. The sets are marked by the variables noted above: tempo, texture, types of rhythm sections or grooves, the stylistic coherence of the most prominent samples, and broader musical themes and motifs that reappear throughout the album.

A Work in Five Sets

Rather than continue any further micro-level narration of the rest of the album through the structure, timing, prominence, and interplay of the musical materials, I'd like to leave that task and expand our scope slightly. I'd like to lay out the rest of the album based on the major section changes (see Figure 3). The goal is to then move to a broader look at the medium that made this album so meaningful for so many for such a long time.

Set 2 begins right at the start of "Flight Tonight." The mood suddenly shifts to an up tempo dance track reminiscent of early Detroit techno. The beat is defined by a strong, unsyncopated sixteenth-note beat with clean percussion sounds that start by playing around on and off the beat, not just on two and four. It then settles into a strong four-on-the-floor with bright, clattering drums holding it down. The mood has suddenly turned to urgency. This tempo and rhythmic style persist for nearly six minutes. Then, while the mood repeatedly edges toward calm in "Close to You," it then swells back into its dance floor drive again. It finally dissipates in the first half of "Diners Only" only to gradually start pushing again in the second half. A vibrant blast of muted horns starts the disco-tinge of "A Different Feeling," which keeps its smooth grooves and common tempo almost to the start of "Electricity." But just a touch before the track change, we are clearly moving to a new mood. Sure enough, by about 3.30 of "A Different Feeling," Set 3 starts to stir. At about 4.07, the beat finally, reluctantly cedes the floor and "Electricity" begins with something akin to an angelic choir. After an appropriate pause for breath, the beat reemerges as mid-tempo, early 1970s funk.[22] The urgency of the previous tracks has been smoothed over, but not quite abandoned. "Electricity" moves like a Bell Curve, working up into a groove and then easing right back out of it again at the opposite point on the other side of the slope. The angels reappear and out of the mist comes Nancy Wilson, of all people, singing the words of the title of the next track, "Tonight May Have to Last Me All My Life." We've exited the dance floor into the rear lounge and are being entertained by a piano, singer, and vibraphone as the third set ambles to its close.

The gestures that follow this mood of quiet repose are a genuine surprise. While we had a few sound effects played for comic effect earlier on the album, they roar back with a vengeance for the entirety of Set 4. The vibraphone is rudely usurped by the low moan of ship's horn, and "Pablo's Cruise" slowly rouses itself from a hush to the rush of a seaside carousel, seagulls, and another blast of the horn, this time much louder. Then perhaps the most anomalous, yet strangely apt track on the whole album begins. With a rumble of horses coming right at us from out of an old time Western, we are confronted with the unalloyed strangeness of "Frontier Psychiatrist." As the horse we heard ages ago whinnies again right in front of us, we are taken into what sounds like a principal's office to catch a fraught conversation between a worried mother and a stern educator. Dexter (heh heh) is out of hand and is about to be expelled from the entire Baltimore public school system. Cue the dramatic choir, swaying back and forth in full voice in the

---

[22] "Rapp Dirty" by Blowfly (1973).

minor key as we are rhythmically regaled repeatedly with all the ways in which Dexter is "crazy in the coconut." The track is a comedy for the overwrought and we'll revisit it momentarily when we talk about its accompanying video. It's a tough act to follow and it's probably for the best that the next track doesn't really try.

Set 5 starts right at beginning of "ETOH" and for the next eighteen minutes or so, we are gradually, carefully guided to the end of the album. "ETOH" and "Summer Cranes" present us with a lightness and space that we had only heard in auditory glimpses before this. Now, we have almost ten minutes of easy textures, consonant tones, and subdued beats. The extraordinary richness of oddly soft timpani and rich vibrant strings has soaked itself in the endless reverb reminiscent of a Walker Brothers ballad. While this might feel like the last few moments of energy, we are in for one last surprise. Part way through "Little Journey," we can just start to hear the bassline from "Holiday" again. It's back, but this time it's as if we are hearing it through a wall between us and a party. If we follow the consensus narrative presented in the previous chapter, then we can imagine that "Live at Dominos" has suddenly veered into one last attempt to get everybody back on the dance floor and for about five minutes we're moving and we're grooving and it's fabulous. But we know it can't last, no matter how ingratiating the beats might be. With about fifteen seconds left in the track, it all eases to a stop, the beats having exhausted themselves despite their best efforts and repeated hints at revival. The final track on the album, "Extra Kings," seems to be telling us that the sun is coming up over the sea and we need to go home, and let all the energy and drama of the night eventually fade into sleep.

A Multiplicity of Contingent Works

If we return to the ideas of the medium and materials of *Since I Left You*, we have to face up to the fact that there isn't just one *Since I Left You*. There are many. From the moment the first early mixes and bootlegs started circulating, something we now call *Since I Left You* started approaching. When it arrived, it wasn't quite the same as it was when it was first made public. Also, it didn't stop changing after its official release. This is all perfectly in keeping with the medium that made these materials aesthetically meaningful. Sample-based music of the type The Avalanches make is part of a long tradition of music making that doesn't simply *tolerate* multiple versions of the same work; it depends on them. It depends on their circulation for works to accrue meaning and value. Versions elicit feedback and emendation. They let the makers think about what they've done and change tack if necessary. And they often let the "right" people know what they are doing and where they are going with it. We saw this in the last chapter.

As such, in a fundamental sense, the version of *Since I Left You* most of us got to hear was simply one contingency in a series of them. This is not to say it is not somehow definitive. It is. But in order to understand it more thoroughly, it helps if we briefly peer into the history of the different versions of the materials that made up this album and their various permutations. To close out this chapter, I will look at a few moments in the lives of different iterations of some of the materials from this work that tell us something about both its specificity and contingency. From this, we will also move into an analysis of what we might call ancillary media, in this case the music videos for the tracks "Since I Left You" and "Frontier Psychiatrist." Both have had interesting lives over the past couple of decades that can bring us to some understanding of how the meaning of this album has changed. We will end this chapter with a summation of the medium and meaning of this work on the occasion of its twentieth anniversary.

In the years before the official release of the album in the UK and the US, the band produced a whole series of live and recorded mixes for limited circulation. Four in particular tell us a lot about the specificity of the album that would eventually become "the work." One of the earlier mixes we can learn from was referred to as GIMIX, produced as a promotional cassette in July 2000. It has since achieved wide distribution through means we will look at shortly. The band's original Australian record label, Modular, produced it in an attempt to get a little bit ahead of the bootlegs and demos that had begun circulating widely, especially in London. It begins straightforwardly, with a slightly different mix of "Since I Left You." It continues along the path eventually forged in the first five or so minutes of the album it would eventually become. Even Madonna turns up where she's expected. But then at about 5.02, someone unexpected arrives, Bob Dylan, and he kind of overstays his welcome. We hear the Nobel bard rhythmically intoning the initial verse of "Like A Rolling Stone" in perfect time with Madonna's rhythm section. Notably, "Holiday" actually cuts out and we are left almost completely alone with Bob for about half a minute. Unlike the vast majority of samples on the official album which are completely unrecognizable, we have two extremely high-profile samples that coincide. After "Holiday's" bassline and drum track return and Bob takes his leave, things briefly return to normal, in this case with the minor key samba of "Stay Another Season" accompanied by the horse. We then move into "Two Hearts in 3/4 Time" for its entirety, but then, instead of the party rap of "Flight Tonight," we get a different inflection on 1980s and early 1990s hip hop, with a deft melding of De La Soul's nostalgia trip "A Roller Skating Jam Named 'Saturdays'" and Blowfly's "Rapp Dirty." Then, things get strange, with Ol' Dirty Bastard jamming with Roy Ayers and Kid Creole, while Jimi Hendrix and Cyndi Lauper then follow on from one another.

What's important to understand about this mix is the bold, if not aggressive, manipulation of one classic song after another, including Deee-Lite's "Groove Is in the Heart," Michael Jackson's "Billie Jean," and comical renderings of "Sgt. Pepper's Lonely Hearts Club Band" and Men at Work's "Down Under" (which might as well be Australia's Sgt Pepper's). When members of the music press referred to the band as "cheeky antipodeans," this is what they meant (Gleeson, 2001). There are two aspects to The Avalanches practice that are present here that are worth noting. First, this mix is far more indebted to the classic version of the mash-up that any subsequent official release would be. This is not surprising as 2000 was probably the absolute peak of the mash-up as a form. The band has noted the influence of mash-ups on many occasions. The flat, open tension between source recordings found here is particularly blatant and is the defining feature of the mash-up. This is precisely what is absent on the "real" album. In fact, the album possesses an almost uncannily seamless coherence and rarely if ever produces such obvious contrasts. Second, not only are a huge number of the samples on the GIMIX mix easy to recognize; stylistically they clearly bear the influence of DJ Dexter, whose DMC routines traded heavily in the historical resonances of classic rock.

The second version is from Australia's national "youth" broadcaster Triple JJJ from August 2001. It was a live set credited to DJ Dexter on the occasion of his fourth Australian DMC Championship success. Characteristically, it starts with Hendrix. Mirroring his DMC routines, he scratches the opening riff to "Purple Haze" crafting a crazy quilt of snatches from the song. Following this is a mangled Louis Armstrong underpinned by the Jurassic Five, after which we are finally allowed to hear something from the "new" album in the form of "Frontier Psychiatrist." As with the GIMIX, we find mostly the materials again often mixed and scratched within an inch of their sonic lives.

The final two mixes were produced for the BBC Radio 1 program "Breezeblock," in February 2001, one of the most influential programs of its kind, and by Cornerstone Promotions, the PR firm of founders of the magazine *The Fader*, the latter dating from November 2001. The "Breezeblock" set begins with almost unadorned clips of Crosby Stills and Nash's "Just a Song Before I Go" and The Beach Boys' "The Trader." I say almost as there are seagulls in the background. The "Cornerstone" set begins with The Beach Boys' "Cool, Cool Water" and is followed by Van Dyke Parks and Arthur Lyman. Each set mirrors the other as both wind their ways through the kinds of music that would seem to be almost anathema to the kinds of dance music coursing through Sydney and London at the time. Each set, both part of a very successful and up front marketing campaign, seems to almost sneer at the deep bass and hardcore beats prevalent among the dance music elite in cities that certainly thought of themselves as centers of the known musical universe at that time. And yet these meandering sets of sunshine and seagulls captured the fancy of more than a few in the know, as noted in the last chapter.

These charming, disarming mixes were full of sounds that were almost alien to most listeners at that time. They were not meant to hit hard and fast. In some ways they did the opposite. As Chater told Steve Bell, while he was working on the album, he quickly realized, like, it's going to take me a lifetime to make drums that hit as hard as say, Lock Off and Beats or something like that. Like that is a whole craft in and of itself. And I don't want to kind of be like second best at something like that. So it was a conscious decision to shift a little and make go with a lighter sound. So we were sampling all these strange old 60s records, anyway, that had no bass in them and they had soft drums.

(Bell, 2021)

These sets are a product of that decision, one that clearly paid off. These sets were about two of the most important skills in this musical tradition, choosing source materials and listening to them in very specific ways that their manipulation makes manifest. These manipulations had to be done skillfully and effectively in order to establish a personally distinct way of presenting these to the audience.

Taken in sum, there is no way one could really anticipate what *Since I Left You* would really sound like, but that's precisely my point. The album went far beyond any of these early mixes in terms of the seamless melding of source materials into a coherent and unified whole. In fact, the retreat from the tension and snark typical of the mash-up is what made the official album so different from most of what the band had been doing up to that point and to some extent what others had been doing in this tradition of practice as well. Not coincidently, this is what it has been most praised for ever since, its "freshness." We can take this and move more or less in a straight line to the unexpectedly vibrant twentieth anniversary of what had become by then an officially "Great Album."

The medium that made the materials of this album meaningful changed out of almost all recognition between 2002 and 2020. Among the more interesting aspects of this post-official release history are two music videos for "Since I Left You" and "Frontier Psychiatrist." Both expertly complemented and extended the music. The video for "Since I Left You" begins with two portly coal miners, in seeming nineteenth-century dress, sitting glumly underground, trapped by a cave in. Then, they hear the start of the song, muted, above them. They start pulling down a section of the roof of the mine to find the source. They push on what they find is a trap door and the light from the room and sound of the music covers them. They are met by two female ballet dancers decked out in 1980s dance gear. They appear to be auditioning for a row of judges. The scene recalls nothing so much as the climactic scene from *Flashdance*. The older of the two miners walks into the performance space and, after a moment of confusion, gets his bearings and immediately begins to dance, slightly comically at first, and then joins in a routine that eventually synchronizes almost perfectly with the two dancers. The young miner remains off to the side, smiling and moving awkwardly in unsuccessful imitation. Eventually, the younger man is ineluctably drawn back into the past from which they had both just emerged, while his colleague stays in the fantasy world. The final scene shows us the younger man, now old, explaining that "Three days later they dug me out. I never saw Arthur again. But wherever he's gone, I'll bet he's having a damn good time." The clip perfectly captures the balance of joy and melancholy of the song. The video won Video of the Year at the 2001 MTV Europe Music Awards. As of December 2023, the video had been on the band's official YouTube channel for fourteen years and had garnered fifteen million views.

The video for "Frontier Psychiatrist" also captures the nature of a very different song. As noted, this is the biggest musical anomaly on the album. The song is riddled with over the top and ridiculous samples from all manner of films and sound recordings. The video maps and mirrors nearly all of these visually. In many cases, they are acted out by unknown actors. In its entirety, the video is a fascinatingly bizarre and unsettling comic panoply of the very kinds of scraps and pieces that comprise the song itself, but in this case, all are mimed in a disturbingly intense and over the top way. The setting is a retro stage reminding one of an old-time television variety show. The entirety of the "cast" we hear in the song stand and wait to "perform" their parts. At one point, when the sample of the song "Ski-Surfing" by 1960s surf rock group The Avalanches comes on, someone rolls a huge disc of The 45 across the stage. Goofy doesn't begin to describe it, but effective does. The video is an excellent representation of the era of the mash-up. As of December 2023, the video had been on the band's official YouTube channel for fourteen years and had garnered twenty-four million views.

My purpose in describing these videos is to close this chapter with an extremely brief explanation of how the medium of this album had changed between 2003 and 2020. When the initial flush of success The Avalanches experienced had faded, we were not yet in a world with iPhones, iTunes, or Spotify, nor did we have easily accessible streamed sound files just randomly distributed across the internet. In the ten or so years preceding their twentieth-anniversary reissue of *Since I Left You*, the band had not ignored how the world of music consumption was changing. They posted videos on YouTube fairly early in the game and it paid off handsomely. Their earliest videos have more or less been available as long as YouTube has been around. Similarly, unlike some in the music industry, the band clearly understood the benefit of their work circulating widely and continuously. Through such comparatively obscure things such as Reddit groups and DJ mix sites, the band's work has been continuously accessible despite their comparative inability to produce a follow-up in what some might consider a timely manner. Part of their extraordinary renown is due in large part to people within the online worlds of sample-based music who refused to let this album fade into obscurity. In my work on this book, I have found multiple websites that have claimed to have produced the master list of samples from *Since I Left You*. They haven't, of course. But I have found multiple videos which expertly link the sources the band used to their appearance on the album, with one YouTube producer meticulously noting every tone and tempo change in every prominent scrap of sound on the album.

In short, the internet culture that has grown up around sampled-based music has given voice to the agency of a fairly wide range of fans of this band. In turn, they have been able to dig up and distribute old mixes, some of the deeply obscure source materials, and, having listened in the same way the band did when they made the album, reverse engineered a significant swathe of it into their YouTube videos and lists of links that have remained active, useful, and accurate for years on end. What I am going to do to conclude this book in the next chapter is to look briefly into how this band and this album have been part of a much larger suite of changes in the world that hasn't just changed how or where or when we listen, but what we actually hear.

Conclusion: The Feels in the Machine

Between the mid-1970s and the mid-1980s, electronic musical instruments such as synthesizers and samplers went from being curios and novelties to being foregrounded for their distinctly non-acoustic, otherworldly sounds. In the decades since, they have gradually become invisibly ubiquitous musical instruments, not usually noticeably different than any other. One of the many debates that attended their long rise to aesthetic normalcy surrounded their "realness," a sometimes pervasive concern that was part of lengthy debates that had been percolating since at least the 1930s. While it is all too easy to look back at the past and mock those who feared "the future," this is a fairly arrogant thing to do. Instead, we should try to understand the content of the fears that once moved on a reluctant parallel path with the clicks, pops, and grinds of the new instruments.

There were at least two things people feared, intuited, and imagined in the new tools that can tell us something of how our world has changed since *Since I Left You* emerged from Melbourne's op shops, junk stores, rock venues, and share houses. One worry was that the labor that went into the construction of musical sound would be devalued or even lost in the sonic mazes that some musicians were making out of music that had already been recorded. No matter how you look at the contemporary music industry, it is almost impossible to see it clearly without also noticing the precipitous extent to which a lot of musical labor has been devalued. You may not want to blame such simple a set of tools as electronic musical instruments for this, but similarly, you still have to admit that they are a central part of a broader circumstance that has seen fit to cheapen the work of the vast majority of musicians, producers, and performers with little apparent hope of restoration. The second worry was that all those ineffable investments of emotion and feeling put into music by musicians would be gradually thinned out until it took the form of the faint aural apparitions of a productive apparatus defined primarily by efficiency and an economic hierarchy that was bound to a consumer culture that only had use for the work of musicians when there was profit to be extracted from it. Again, look around you and tell me this was an entirely false premonition. Yes, I know it's more complicated than that, but still.

My point is that when The Avalanches were working on this album, they were still part of a world in which the value of what they were doing had to be proven both in terms of the work put into it and the feelings taken out of it. It should be obvious by this point in this book that they succeeded on both scores. Rather than rehash this point again, let me just cite one of the more prominent converts from the old school of music writing, Nick Hornby. His complaint concerned the authentic accomplishment of sample-based music. "I once presumed that nothing good—nothing great, anyway—could come out of the mixing and matching and scratching and cutting and pasting," he wrote. While such works "remained essentially plagiaristic, [they] accomplished nothing." However, he thought The Avalanches were different. They used "scraps of things you have never heard in ways you couldn't have imagined" and therefore met his elevated standard: "they have, effectively, created something from nothing" (Hornby, 2003: 170–1).

Despite its seeming aesthetic prescience, *Since I Left You* has been said to be great in almost the exact same way most "great works" in popular music have been said to be great. As I have seen fit to remind people, greatness in popular music has routinely been bestowed in ways far more traditional and conservative than almost anyone seems to realize. In fact, I have long taken great delight in pointing out to my colleagues, peers, and students that the work of everyone from Joni Mitchell to Led Zeppelin to Kendrick Lamar to Beyoncé has been celebrated as "great" in pretty much the same way (Fairchild, 2021, 2024). Remarkably, the cardinal directions of this vision of artistic greatness were defined by no less an eminence than the poet and essayist T. S. Eliot in a brief missive from 1957. Eliot wrote that a great work should have gravitas, seriousness of intent, intellectual maturity, artistic or formal maturity, and a superlative form of emotional expression and impact. It should also endure and be subject to imitation (Eliot, 1957). The form of greatness attributed to this album remains grounded in precisely these attributes which have long been persistent in the ways in which some works of popular music have been elevated beyond the mere world that made them. Now only one piece of the puzzle of attributed greatness needs to be slotted into place: the legacy.

There are more than a few musicians who have pointed to this album and told us how much it meant to them, especially in Australia. After the turn of the century, Australia was said to have experienced a "golden age of band-driven electronic music." We were told that it "peaked with chart-topping releases from The Presets and Cut Copy" and included "albums from Pnau, Van She and Midnight Juggernauts to strengthen the scene's vital power" (Carbines, 2021). Perhaps unsurprisingly, most of the bands receiving such accolades were part of the Modular Recordings universe of production, performance, and promotion, the label on which The Avalanches first released *Since I Left You*. When the history of this cozy world was written, it was in tones that should be familiar to us by now:

> Key players point to The Avalanches' ground-breaking 2000 album "Since I Left You", one of Modular's first releases, as a turning point, the first motion of what would become a movement at the start of the new millennium. This was what Australian electronic music could be: interesting and internationally acclaimed.
>
> (Carbines, 2021)

Our old friend Stephen Pavlovic is routinely cited as the driving force behind this second generation of international success stories. The story of how one band, Cut Copy, got their start should sound familiar. "There was no live electronic scene to speak of in Melbourne," we were told, "so Cut Copy cut their teeth playing on bills with punk and rock bands." Band members said that this "honed their energetic live shows—they had to be compelling as stylistic fish out of water" (Carbines, 2021).

These bands also spoke of "a supportive community of kindred spirits" of venues, events, and audiences that embraced each other forming a diverse community in which "there weren't any kinds of barriers anymore" (Carbines, 2021). Once again, the British came calling and the multinational promotions machine greased the gears for another set of young, ambitious artists. This should be a familiar formula by now. But there was one important difference: these newer bands had a medium that was very different than the one that helped *Since I Left You* make its mark. This movement:

began with the ripples of artists experimenting turned into waves after 2000, when the internet allowed these acts to find fans and be heard everywhere for the first time—Cut Copy unveiling "Hearts On Fire" on Myspace before they'd finished "In Ghost Colours". It washed over the globe, establishing communities of Australian artists in all the major hubs and made electronic music, live and otherwise, the norm.

(Carbines, 2021)

According to those who have championed this electro pop underground, this was a form of music that wasn't defined by "a cohesive sound but how you found the music." This was music that was suited to a new medium: "low-quality MP3s … disseminated on the fly by artists, creating an ever-growing treasure trove of new tracks, remixes and mash-ups" that would be taken to the audience through online hookups, underground dance parties, and free downloads (Cunningham, 2021). Australian artists were able to infiltrate these new international online networks as their music hit with a new potency as part of a global wave of emotional and emotive electronic pop definitively shaped by the oddly late EDM boom in the United States that began in the late 2000s. It surged into the mainstream, taking it over almost entirely. This so-called golden age of Australian electro pop was ostentatiously hedonistic and self-absorbed, joyful and sardonic, deeply self-aware of its own lack of "seriousness" (Cunningham, 2021).

The Avalanches made an album that was pushed into a circulatory system of bootlegs, message boards, magazine articles, and alternative mixes that was just on the precipice of dissolution and reformation. When music blogs, MP3 downloads, and the strange immediacy of online social connection transformed these tools with a new speed, intensity, and emotional impact, the status and meaning of this album changed. *Since I Left You* has benefited mightily from being produced in one paradigm, a very nearly analog one, but finding its staying power in another, a newly digitalized one. The meticulous work that made the album itself, with all of its varied fragments, sections, sets, and tracks, was perfectly suited to the routine acts of assembly, disassembly, reconstruction, and versioning that the tradition of sample-based music had already relied on for its success.

The long rich afterlife of this work was founded in large part on a new feelings-based culture of assessment and consideration of new music. Rather than cohering around musical genres or styles or traditions, new cultures of popular music consumption coalesced around styles of social connection and expression. The joy and verve of the music The Avalanches made, both its simultaneous ease and intensity of feeling, were unwittingly purpose-built for a new world of deliberative pleasure-seeking and purposeful indulgence. It was produced in a culture of popular music in Australia that had long embraced and loved the fizz and joy of hedonic pop, but also embraced the dirt and sweat of the local indie rock venue. *Since I Left You* is a mélange of sources, sounds, feelings, techniques, skills, and ideals. It grabbed its champions and fans from the start with its mystery and mundanity, its ethereal atmospheres and textured immediacy. It is in these senses that this band and this album extended the world of popular music just far enough to make sure it included them, and there is no doubt that it still does.

Bibliography

Adams, Cameron (2001) "Spin Drift." *The Courier-Mail*, 22 March, p. 40.

Adams, Cameron (2000) "When Seconds Count." *The Courier-Mail*, 8 December, p. 6.

Arrow, Michelle (2009) *Friday on Our Minds: Popular Culture in Australia since 1945*. Sydney: New South Press.

"Artzone: The Avalanches" (1999) Film Australia.

Aston, Martin (2001) "Album Choice: The Avalanches Since I Left You." *The Times*, p. 10.

Barkham, Patrick (2001) "Friday Review: Cut Up and Dance." *The Guardian*, 13 April, p. 16.

Bell, Steve (2021) "An Oral History of the Avalanches Since I Left You." Rewind with Steve Bell. https://open.spotify.com/episode/1tvnD2Wj388JbWncQRwWGT. Accessed on November 16, 2023.

Bennun, David (2020) "Been Around the World: The Magical Odyssey of The Avalanches' Since I Left You." *The Quietus*, 23 November. https://thequietus.com/articles/29262-avalanches-since-i-left-you-review-anniversary. Accessed on March 23, 2023.

Bollen, Jonathan (2013) "Show Girls and Choreographers in Australian Entertainment: The Transition to Nightclubs, 1946–1967." *Australasian Drama Studies*, 63, pp. 52–68.

Bongiorno, Frank (2015) *The Eighties: The Decade That Transformed Australia*. Collingwood: Black Inc.

Brewster, Bill, and Frank Broughton (1999) *Last Night a DJ Saved My Life: The History of the Disc Jockey*. New York: Grove Press.

Burgess, John (2001) "Aussie Rules." *Jockey Slut*, April. https://www.discopogo.co/archive/aussie-rules-the-avalanches. Accessed on November 23, 2023.

Cahill, Mikey (2016) "The Avalanches Have Conquered Health Issues, Lawsuits, Lost Funds and Empire of the Sun to Bloom Again with Wildflower." *News.com.au*, 11 July. https://www.news.com.au/entertainment/music/tours/the-avalanches-have-conquered-health-issues-lawsuits-lost-funds-and-empire-of-the-sun-to-bloom-again-with-wildflower/news-story/d550cbd79fca08274ecd28887c5f518b. Accessed on November 22, 2023.

Carbines, Scott (2021) "'Everything Just Collapsed into Everything': Australia's Golden Age of Electronic Music." *Mixmag*, 18 January. https://mixmag.net/feature/australia-golden-age-electronic-music-sydney-melbourne-modular-gang-bang. Accessed on October 11, 2023.

Coleman, Jonny (2016) "Meet the Woman Who Helps The Beastie Boys, Beck and The Avalanches Clear Their Samples." *The LA-ist*, 18 October. https://laist.com/news/entertainment/pat-shannahan-detective-sampling-interview. Accessed on November 22, 2023.

Cozijn, John (1983) "Comment." *Campaign*, 95(November), p. 6.

Creswell, Toby (2003) *Love Is In the Air: Stories of Australian Pop*. DVD. Australia: Australian Broadcasting Corporation.

Cunningham, Katie (2021) "'Everyone Was Partying for Their Life': Bang Gang, Bloghouse and the Indie Sleaze of the Mid-2000s." *The Guardian*, 18 December. https://www.theguardian.com/music/2021/dec/18/everyone-was-partying-for-their-life-bang-gang-bloghouse-and-the-indie-sleaze-of-the-mid-2000s. Accessed on October 18, 2023.

Dean, Jodi (2023) "Feudalism by Design: On Quinn Slobodian's 'Crack-Up Capitalism.'" *Los Angeles Review of Books*, 10 April. https://lareviewofbooks.org/article/feudalism-by-design-on-quinn-slobodians-crack-up-capitalism/. Accessed on December 20, 2023.

Denning, Michael (2015) *Noise Uprising: The Audiopolitics of a World Musical Revolution*. London: Verso.

Deville, Chris (2020) "*Since I Left You* Turns 20." *Stereogum*, 27 November. https://www.stereogum.com/2108230/avalanches-since-i-left-you/reviews/the-anniversary/. Accessed on November 21, 2023.

DJ Shadow (1996) *Endtroducing . . .* Mo'Wax. 697-124 123-2.

Donovan, Patrick (2001a) "Sticky Carpet." *The Age*, 23 February, p. 5.

Donovan, Patrick (2001b) "Feature Single of the Week." *The Age*, 16 February, p. 7.

Donovan, Patrick (2001c) "How Some Blokes from Brunswick Won Britain in a Landslide." *The Age*, 5 October, p. 13.

Donovan, Patrick, and Anthony Carew (2000) "Sampling the Big Time." *The Age*, 1 December, p. 12.

Duffy, Michael (2001) "Watertight Future." *The Advertiser* (Adelaide), 25 January, p. 44.

Duffy, Michael (2000) "Imagine There's No Single." *The Advertiser* (Adelaide), 5 October, p. 46.

Ediriwira, Amar (2016) "Since I Left You: How The Avalanches Weaved Thousands of Samples into a Supernatural Tapestry." *The Vinyl Factory*, 2 June. https://thevinylfactory.com/features/the-avalanches-since-i-left-you/. Accessed on November 13, 2023.

Eliezer, Christie (2001) "The Year in Music 2001: The Year in Australia." *Billboard*, 29 December/5 January, p. YE18.

Eliot, T. S. (1957) *On Poetry and Poets*. London: Faber and Faber.

Enis, Eli (2020) "Everything in Its Right Place: How a Perfect 10.0 Review of Radiohead's 'Kid A' Changed Music Criticism 20 Years Ago." *Billboard*, 26 March. https://www.billboard.com/articles/columns/rock/9342543/radiohead-kid-a-pitchfork-review-brent-discrescenzo-2000. Accessed on July 28, 2021.

Fairchild, Charles (2024) *The Capitalist Imaginaries of Popular Music*. Bristol: Intellect Books.

Fairchild, Charles (2021) *Musician in the Museum: Display and Power in Neoliberal Popular Culture*. New York: Bloomsbury Academic.

Fairchild, Charles (2014) *Danger Mouse's The Grey Album*. New York: Bloomsbury Academic.

Fenwick, Julie (2022) "An Oral History of the Rise and Fall of Sydney's Once-Magical Club Scene." *Vice*, 31 May. https://www.vice.com/en/article/xgdekw/an-oral-history-of-the-rise-and-fall-of-sydneys-once-magical-club-scene. Accessed on October 11, 2023.

Ferguson, Jordan (2014) *J Dilla's Donuts*. New York: Bloomsbury Academic.

Forde, Eamonn (2006) "Conflict and Collaboration: The Press Officer/Journalist Nexus in the British Music Press of the Late 1990s." *Popular Music History*, 1(3), pp. 285–306.

Forde, Eamonn (2001) "From Polyglottism to Branding: On the Decline of Personality Journalism in the British Music Press." *Journalism*, 2(1), pp. 23–43.

Galbraith, Larry (1986) "The Business of Gay Parties." *OutRage*, 34(March), pp. 20–2.

Geertz, Clifford (2000) "The World in Pieces: Culture and Politics at the End of the Century." In *Available Light: Anthropological Reflections on Philosophical Topics*. Princeton, NJ: Princeton University Press, pp. 218–63.

Gleeson, Sinéad (2001) "The Avalanches—Since I Left You." *RTE*, 19 April. https://www.rte.ie/entertainment/music-reviews/2001/0419/448431-avalanches/. Accessed on November 23, 2023.

Gonsher, Aaron (2016) "Sample Clearance Expert Pat 'The Detective' Shannahan Is The Avalanches' Secret Weapon." *Red Bull Music Academy Daily*, 18 August. https://daily.redbullmusicacademy.com/2016/08/pat-the-detective-shannahan-interview. Accessed on November 13, 2023.

Gracyk, Theodore (1996) *Rhythm and Noise: An Aesthetics of Rock*. Durham, NC: Duke University Press.

Hall, Rashaun (2001) "Cornerstone Launches Management Division." *Billboard*, 15 December, p. 6.

Harley, Ross, and Andrew Murphie (2007) "Rhythms and Refrains: A Brief History of Australian Electronica." *Culture Machine*, p. 9. https://culturemachine.net/recordings/rhythms-and-refrains/. Accessed on October 12, 2023.

Herbert, Conor (2021) "Celebrating 20 Years of Since I Left You with The Avalanches." *Pilerats*. http://pilerats.com/written/get-to-know/the-avalanches-since-i-left-you-20-years-feature-interview/. Accessed on November 19, 2023.

Herrman, John (2015) "Access Denied." *The Awl*, 3 December. https://www.theawl.com/2015/12/access-denied/. Accessed August 23, 2021.

Holliday, Liz (2021) "Papa Smurf Interview: The History of Melbourne's Rave Scene." *Beat Repeat*, 12 March. https://www.youtube.com/watch?v=zrqDB-np-Q8. Accessed on October 11, 2023.

Holmes, Peter (2000) "Can't Help Standing … for Falling Down." *The Sun-Herald* (Australia), 5 November, p. 12.

Hope, Clover (2015) "Year of the Fanboy Profile." *Jezebel*, 21 December. http://jezebel.com/year-of-the-fanboy-profile-writers-fawning-over-subjec-1748180895. Accessed on July 18, 2016.

Horan, Tom (2001) "Pop CD Reviews." *Daily Telegraph* (London), 21 April.

Hornby, Nick (2003) *31 Songs*. New York: Penguin.

Kent, David (1993) *Australian Chart Book 1970–1992*. St Ives: Australian Chart Book.

Kone, Peter (2001) "The Avalanches: Since I Left you." *Q*, 175(May), p. 102.

LeMay, Matt. (1999) "The Avalanches: Since I Left You." *Pitchfork*, 31 December. https://pitchfork.com/reviews/albums/385-since-i-left-you/. Accessed on February 22, 2022.

Lubinski, Christina (2012) "The Global Business with Local Music: Western Gramophone Companies in India before World War 1." *Bulletin of the GHI*, 51, pp. 67–85.

Luckman, Susan (2002) *Party People: Mapping Contemporary Dance Music Cultures in Australia*. PhD thesis, University of Queensland.

Lynskey, Dorian (2001) "The Avalanches." *Q*, 175(May), p. 34.

Maalsen, Sophia (2019) *The Social Life of Sound*. London: Palgrave Macmillan.

Maksimovic, Semone (2000) "Kings of the Mountain." *The Newcastle Herald* (Australia), 26 October, p. 37.

"Mardi Gras Committee Plans Sleaze Ball" (1982) *Campaign*, 81(September), p. 11.

Mast, Andrew, and Trish Maunder (2000) "Culture Club/Culture Club Profile." *The Age*, p. 13.

McCormick, Peter Dodds (1913) Letter to R.B. Fuller Esq. dated August 1, 1913.

Mengel, Noel (2001) "Exporting Sunshine to the World." *The Courier-Mail*, 24 November, p. M08.

Murphie, Andrew, and Edward Scheer (1992) "Dance Parties: Capital, Culture, and Simulation." In Philip Hayward (ed.) *From Pop to Punk to Postmodernism: Popular Music and Australian Culture from the 1960s to the 1990s*. Sydney: Allen & Unwin, pp. 172–84.

National Library of Australia (2011) *Who'll Come a Waltzing Matilda with Me?* https://webarchive.nla.gov.au/awa/20110606173517/http://pandora.nla.gov.au/pan/34755/20110606-1326/www.nla.gov.au/epubs/waltzingmatilda/index.html. Accessed on December 19, 2023.

Nell and Noona (1987) "Feature by Noona and Nell." *OutRage*, 52 (September), p. 21.

Olson, Catherine Applefield (2002) "Shortlist Lengthens Promotional Scope." *Billboard*, 2 November, p. 65.

Paoletta, Kyle (2019) "For All Fankind." *The Baffler*, September. https://thebaffler.com/outbursts/for-all-fankind-paoletta. Accessed on July 28, 2021.

Paoletta, Michael (2001) "Avalanches Start a Landslide with London-Sire US Release." *Billboard*, 13 October, p. 40.

Park, Michael, and Gareth Northwood (1996) "Australian Dance Culture." *Ohms Not Bombs*. https://ohmsnotbombs.net/sporadical/australian-dance-culture-by-michael-park-gareth-northwood. Accessed on October 1, 2023.

Petridis, Alexis (2016) "'We Lost Our Minds'—How The Avalanches Spent the Last 16 Years." *The Guardian*, 15 July. https://www.theguardian.com/music/2016/jul/14/the-avalanches-wildflower-interview. Accessed on March 23, 2023.

Poe, Jim (2017) "Oral History of the Sydney Rave Scene, 1989–1994." *Red Bull*, 18 January. https://www.redbull.com/au-en/

oral-history-of-the-sydney-rave-scene-1989-1994. Accessed on November 6, 2023.

Price, Simon (2001) "The Joy of Segues—With the Osmonds for Dessert." *The Independent on Sunday*, 12 August, p. 11.

Rasmus, Jack (2020) *The Scourge of Neoliberalism: US Economic Policy from Reagan to Trump*. Atlanta, GA: Clarity Press.

Reese, Henry Peter (2019) *Colonial Soundscapes: A Cultural History of Sound Recording in Australia, 1880–1930*. PhD thesis, University of Melbourne.

Reynolds, Simon (2001) "The Avalanches: Since I Left You." *Spin*. https://www.spin.com/2016/07/review-the-avalanches-since-i-left-you/. Accessed on November 23, 2023.

Richards, Sam (2011) "My Favourite Album: Since I Left You by The Avalanches." *The Guardian*, 20 August. https://www.theguardian.com/music/musicblog/2011/aug/19/favourite-album-avalanches. Accessed on March 23, 2023.

Scatena, Dino (2001) "Tide Turing for Innovative Music." *Daily Telegraph* (Australia), 12 September, p. 31.

Seligman, Craig (2023) "Yes, Sydney, Australia in the 1960s Was the Drag Capital of the World." *Literary Hub*, 3 March. https://lithub.com/yes-sydney-australia-in-the-1960s-was-the-drag-capital-of-the-world/. Accessed on October 20, 2023.

Seymour, Richard (2019) *The Twittering Machine*. London: The Indigo Press.

Shanahan, Brendan (2001) "Pop Goes the DJ." *The Weekend Australian*, 13 January, p. 1.

Shepherd, Fiona (2001) "Sampling the Delights." *The Scotsman*, p. 8.

Stafford, Andrew (2004) *Pig City: From the Saints to Savage Garden*. St Lucia: University of Queensland Press.

Steele, Alice (n.d.) "The History of King's Cross." *Sky Sirens*. https://www.skysirens.com.au/the-history-of-kings-cross. Accessed on October 20, 2023.

Stewart, Gary (2000) *Rumba on the River: A History of the Popular Music of the Two Congos*. London: Verso.

St. John, Graham (2001) "Doof! Australian Post-Rave Culture." In Graham St John (ed.) *FreeNRG: Notes from the Edge of the Dance Floor*. Melbourne: Common Ground, pp. 9–36.

Stockbridge, Sally (1992) "Rock Music on Australian 'TV.'" In Philip Hayward (ed.) *From Pop to Punk to Postmodernism: Popular Music and Australian Culture from the 1960s to the 1990s*. Sydney: Allen & Unwin, pp. 68–85.

Stratton, Jon (2020) "The Scientists, *Blood Red River* (1983)." In Jon Stratton and Jon Dale (eds.) *An Anthology of Australian Albums: Critical Engagements*. London: Bloomsbury Academic, pp. 53–66.

Stratton, Jon (2018) "The Birthday Party and the Scientists: Nihilism, Suburbia and the Importance of Class." *Thesis Eleven*, 144(1), pp. 100–16.

Stratton, Jon (2007) *Australian Rock: Essays on Popular Music*. Perth: Network Books.

Sullivan, Peter (2001) "Wizards of Oz." *Muzik*, 77(October), pp. 60–6.

"The Avalanches Break Down Their Favorite Samples" (2021) *Under the Influences*, 22 June. https://pitchfork.com/video/watch/the-avalanches-under-the-influences. Accessed on December 4, 2023.

Tomazin, Farrah (2000) "Suits Go Feral." *The Age*, 24 November.

Warren, Emma (2001) "The Avalanches: Since I Left You." *The Face*, 3(50), pp. 156–9.

Wilder, Eliot (2005) *DJ Shadow's Entroducing ...* New York: Bloomsbury Academic.

Zak, Albin (2010) *I Don't Sound Like Nobody: Remaking Music in 1950s America*. Ann Arbor, MI: University of Michigan Press.

Zuel, Bernard (2021) "The Avalanches—Since I Left You 20th Anniversary Edition." https://www.bernardzuel.net/post/the-avalanches-since-i-left-you-20th-anniversary-edition-review. Accessed on March 26, 2023.

Zuel, Bernard (2014) "Albert Productions, the Label Behind AC/DC, Rocks up 50 Years." *Sydney Morning Herald*, 10 August. https://www.smh.com.au/entertainment/music/albert-productions-the-label-behind-acdc-rocks-up-50-years-20140807-1018kh.html. Accessed on 10 June 2023.

Index

"Advance Australia Fair" 15, 17, 19
The Age (Melbourne) 61
Albert Productions 21
Australian Music Report (Kent Music Report) 28
Australian Recording Industry Association (ARIA) x, 28, 34, 53

Beastie Boys, The 40, 42, 46, 50, 51, 62
Bell, Steve 37, 38, 40, 41, 43, 44, 47, 48, 49, 50, 51, 65, 72, 73, 81, 82, 83, 98
"bush doofs" 33–4

Chater, Robby 38, 39, 40–7, 50, 65, 72, 74, 81–3, 98
Cold War, The 3–4
colonialism 16
Cornerstone Productions 48, 98
"cultural cringe" 14

Danger Mouse 5
Dawson, Peter 19
Denning, Michael 16–17, 23
Di Blasi, Tony 39, 43, 44, 82
DJ Shadow 5–7, 40
Donuts 8–9

EDM (electronic dance music) xii, 14, 23–4, 33–4, 68, 103–7
Espie, Tony 47–9, 50

Fabay, Dexter (DJ Dexta) 39, 43, 45, 61, 68, 97
The Face 61, 65–7, 68, 69
Ferguson, Jordan 8–9
Forde, Eamonn 58

"gay parties" 30, 32
Girl Talk 5, 74
Gracyk, Theodore 78–9
gramophones 16, 23
greatness 56–7, 60, 70, 105
The Guardian 65, 73

J Dilla 5, 8
Jockey Slut 66, 68–9

Lubinski, Christina 16

Maalsen, Sophia 7
Madlib 5
Madonna 27, 56, 61, 62, 67, 81, 85, 96
McCormack, Peter Dodds 17
Modular Recordings 45, 48, 96, 106
MTV 53, 100

Mushroom Records 40
Muzik 66–7

neoliberalism 4
New Media Strategies 49

Pan Amateurs, The 38–40, 42, 44–5
parlor song 14–15, 20
Patterson, A.B. ("Banjo") 18
Pavolic, Steve 44–6, 48–9, 53, 106
Pitchfork 59, 70, 81
Polizzi, Giovanni 31–2
Public Enemy 46–7, 51

Q Magazine 66–9

Recreational Art Team (RAT) 30–1
Reynolds, Simon 49, 63–4

Saints, The 22, 69
sampling x–xii, 5–7, 9–11, 28, 37, 39–44, 47, 50–3, 60–73, 77–89, 92, 95–104, 108
Scientists, The 22
Seltmann, Darren 39–45
Shannahan, Pat 50–3
sheet music 16–18
Shortlist Music Project 49
Sire Records 48–9
Stratton, Jon 21–2

The Times (London) 62
Triple J x, 97

Vanda and Young 21–2
vernacular music 16–17

"Waltzing Matilda" 15, 17–19
Wilder, Eliot 8

Zak, Albin 20

www.ingramcontent.com/pod-product-compliance
Lightning Source LLC
LaVergne TN
LVHW011905220525
811713LV00007B/22